THE LIMITS OF STORY

THE SOCIETY OF BIBLICAL LITERATURE
SEMEIA STUDIES
Lou H. Silberman, Editor

THE LIMITS OF STORY

George Aichele, Jr.

FORTRESS PRESS
Philadelphia, Pennsylvania

SCHOLARS PRESS
Chico, California

Library of Congress Cataloging in Publication Data

Aichele, George.
   The limits of story.

   (Semeia studies)
   Bibliography: p.
   Includes index.
   1.Discourse analysis, Narrative. 2. Languages—
Philosophy. 3. Literature—Philosophy. 4. Languages—
Religious aspects. 5. Metaphor. I. Title II. Series.
P302.A37   1985   808.3'0141   84–25844
ISBN 0–8006–1513–1 (alk. paper)
ISBN 0–89130–751–6 (Scholars Press : pbk. : alk. paper)

1422A85   Printed in the United States of America   1–1513
on acid-free paper

For Connie, Sara, and Daniel.

CONTENTS

THE LIMITS OF STORY

Everything came to his aid during the construction work. Foreign workers brought the marble blocks, trimmed and fitted to one another. The stones rose and placed themselves according to the gauging motions of his fingers. No building ever came into being as easily as did this temple—or rather, this temple came into being the way a temple should. Except that, to wreak a spite or to desecrate or destroy it completely, instruments obviously of a magnificent sharpness had been used to scratch on every stone—from what quarry had they come?—for an eternity outlasting the temple, the clumsy scribblings of senseless children's hands, or rather the entries of barbaric mountain dwellers.

—Franz Kafka (47)

ACKNOWLEDGEMENT

I owe a great debt to my students, colleagues, and friends for their friendly criticisms and continuing help and encouragement, and especially to Paul de Man, Paul Hessert, Lee Miller, and Lou Silberman.

The epigram to this book is reprinted by permission of Schocken Books, Inc., from *Parables and Paradoxes* by Franz Kafka. Copyright 1935 by Schocken Verlag, Berlin. Copyright 1936, 1937 by Heinr. Mercy Sohn, Prague. Copyright 1946, 1947, 1948, 1953, 1954, 1958 by Schocken Books, Inc. Copyright renewed 1975 by Schocken Books, Inc. Portions of Chapters Five and Six consist of revised and expanded versions of material previously published in *Cross Currents*, Spring, 1981, and Spring, 1983. Copyright 1980, 1983 by Convergence, Inc. Used by permission. The quotation from the prose poetry of Hans Arp is used by permission of Oswald Wolff (Publishers) Ltd., from *Hans Arp, The Poet of Dadaism*, R.W. Last, trans. and ed. Copyright 1969.

NOTE

A number of terms or phrases to be found in this book may not be familiar to the reader. A Glossary, in which some of these terms or phrases are identified, follows Chapter Six. The first time that a term or phrase identified in the Glossary, or its derivative, occurs in each chapter, it will be marked with an asterisk (*).

Chapter One
FRAMES

1. Contexts and Contents

> A name on being mentioned reminds us of the Dresden
> gallery and of our last visit there: we wander through
> the rooms and stand before a picture of Terniers which
> represents a picture gallery. . . . The pictures of the lat-
> ter would in their turn portray pictures which on their
> part exhibited readable inscriptions and so forth. . . .
> (Husserl: 270)

Edmund Husserl uses his memory of the Terniers in the Dresden
gallery as an analogy for a particular complex phenomenon,
"levels in the construction of noesis and noema," and the question of what we mean by the object or content of an experience.
He wishes to argue that every intentional experience—every act
of consciousness—has "a *central 'nucleus'*" of "*sheer 'objective
meaning'*" (246, emphasis Husserl's) which is or can be identical
with the objects of other experiences. Thus the tree that I see
can be the "same" tree as the one that I remember seeing, that I
dreamed about seeing, etc.

Husserl uses the picture to explain how one noematic* object
(the painting in the gallery) may contain, at a different "level,"
another object (the gallery in the painting), and so on, as he says,
ad infinitum. Yet although he says this earlier in the same section (no. 100) of *Ideas,* in his analogy he supposes that the
paintings in the gallery in the painting are themselves the decisive level of noematic construction: they are still lifes, portraits,
landscapes, etc., but eventually they are paintings apparently
about something other than themselves.

However, what if one of those paintings in the painting is
the Terniers? Let us suppose further: what if the entire gallery
in the painting is the very Dresden gallery which contained (for
Husserl) the Terniers? Then we get an infinite regression of
levels of construction, and the noematic object recedes to a

hypothetical point. We see the painting, as a noematic object, but it withdraws infinitely beyond our comprehension.

I am supposing that a painting in the painting is the same painting, and even more, that the gallery in the painting is the same gallery. Whether this was what Husserl saw I do not know, but we can imagine such a situation. Or can we? For we could take the painting off the wall of the gallery and place it in a different location—a different gallery, a house, etc.—but we cannot do this to the gallery itself, nor can we do it to the painting in the painting. The painting can be both physically and noematically separated from its context—the gallery—and its content—the gallery of paintings in it. It is neither what is about it nor what it is about. Neither the paintings nor the gallery in the painting are the same as the "real" painting and the "real" gallery.

The painting (as I have modified it) is infinitely "deep"; it suggests an infinite regression of paintings within paintings. It is also infinitely expansive, for it suggests that the "real" painting and gallery are the contents of yet another picture—moving in the "opposite direction" from the regression "into" the painting—and so on. Husserl notes, for example, that we can recollect at a later time the original experience of viewing the painting in the gallery (271). Only the beholder of the painting remains non-present,* as he or she paces in the gallery, the only one to whom any of it matters, and the very one who can take the painting off the wall and place it elsewhere. The point at which infinite depth and infinite expansion meet is the beholder.

> . . . the double relation of the representation to its model and to its sovereign, to its author as well as to the person to whom it is being offered, this relation is necessarily interrupted. It can never be present without some residuum, even in a representation that offers itself as a spectacle. (Foucault, 1970:16)

Unlike Husserl, who uses his experience in the gallery as an example for his considerations of consciousness, Michel Foucault uses his reflections on Velázquez's *Las Meninas* as an introduction to his considerations of neoclassical understandings of representation.[1] A different sort of relation (or predication) is thereby

---

[1] See also John R. Searle, "*Las Meninas* and the Paradoxes of Pictorial Representation," *Critical Inquiry*, Spring, 1980 (VI, 3), pp. 477–88.

established between the "contents" which these two philosophers offer—the propositions or statements that they make—and the "contexts" to which they point—the paintings on the one hand, and the nature of consciousness and of representation, on the other. (I am not using "content" here in the way that it is sometimes opposed to "form." I hope it is clear that both context and content are formed and may be considered formally.)

Foucault notes that *Las Meninas* reverses the usual arrangement of the portrait. In the painting, the beholder sees the artist standing before his canvas, which has its back to the beholder. Next to the artist are various other persons, most of whom are looking "out" of the painting at the beholder, or rather, at the model of the portrait being painted by the artist in the painting. This model is King Philip IV of Spain and his wife, whose images are reflected in a mirror on the wall of the room portrayed in the painting. The model and the beholder can therefore replace one another in a "ceaseless exchange" of observed (by those in the painting) and observer, an infinite reversal of the invisible (portrait being executed) and the visible (painting which we see) (5).

This exchange is not, however, a binary one. The beholder stands also in the position of the artist—the "real" one, not the one in the picture—as he considers or composes the painting. Reconsidering the passage quoted above, is the "sovereign" of the painting the model (the king) or the painter (the "author")? Is "the person to whom it is being offered" the king or the beholder? Is the "author" the painter or the beholder (considered as any possible viewer for whom it is meaningful) or again the king (who presumably has "authorized" this portrait)? And is the "model" this specific Philip, or the artist as he paints, or anyone in the position of being represented, being viewed and portrayed by others (the beholders in the painting)? Thus Foucault establishes in these four terms an indefinite series of infinite reversals between the poles of artist, model, and beholder. He notes that these three poles are themselves represented in *Las Meninas*, in the self-portrait of Velázquez, in the mirror reflecting the king and his wife, and in an ambiguous figure in the background, apparently undecided whether or not to enter the room where the portrait is being executed—the beholder. The painting itself "doubles" the poles of the ceaseless exchange which is itself absent from it—as the king is absent from *Las Meninas*—and yet incessantly pointed to by it.

This doubling is not quite that of Husserl's depiction of the Terniers. We notice that Foucault's account of the Velázquez allows for neither infinite depth nor infinite expansion. Perhaps if one of the paintings which appear dimly on the walls of the room portrayed in *Las Meninas* was itself *Las Meninas*, then this would be possible. But the depth in *Las Meninas* is the depth of the mirror reflection: a calculable depth, not an infinite one (13). Its expansion into "reality" is, as was noted above, an indefinite one—due to the indefiniteness of the beholder—but it is not an infinite one. Moving the Velázquez would not interfere with the regression of content and context, as it would with Husserl's Terniers (as modified here).

The two infinities of the Terniers (as modified) are two opposite directions in one dimension, meeting at a point which is the beholder. Each infinity is created by a ceaseless regress between content and context, which stand in irreducible opposition to one another and undercut one another. Yet the beholder, the point which establishes the infinite regress, is absent. The two infinities of the Velázquez are "parallel" to one another; they cannot meet. The beholder is caught up in both of the parallel infinities and is therefore not self-identical; yet this parallelism or re-presentation unites the infinities in their opposition. Each one is created by the mutual inter-replaceability of the three poles; thus each one's identity as distinct from the other is also disrupted.

Without attempting to reconcile Husserl's and Foucault's accounts, we can note certain common reverberations: (1) the non-presence of the beholder—not a non-existence or an absence, but a non-presence to which both paintings (and both accounts) point—and (2) the non-identity of the work of art, expressed in infinite oscillation between content and context (the regression of the Terniers) and within the parallels of content and context (the reversals of the Velázquez). This non-identity, oscillation, and undecidability we shall call "self-referentiality."*

2. From the Gallery to the Library

In both of these paintings—and in the comments of Husserl and Foucault, and in my comments—we appear to have examples of what André Malraux calls the suppression of reference which characterizes the contemporary self-awareness of art. Malraux argues that this suppression has coincided with the collecting of works of art into museums and their consequent estrangement from their original function within human culture as a whole (14). The museum moves the art from an original context within the "life" of the culture—the temple, the town plaza, etc.—to a context of deliberate confrontation with other works of art. This opens up the possibility of a theory or criticism of art which seeks those elements common to all art, establishing a history of art, the awareness of artistic types or genres, and most important, the distinction between style and message, between content and context—the self-reflectivity of art as art.

The Terniers and the Velázquez are important to Husserl and Foucault because they simultaneously reflect and challenge this separation, which is essential to modern consciousness and representation. The self-referential interplay between content and context in each work would not be possible if they were not separated. The museum, as the epitome of this separation, is the modern frame par excellence, although Malraux suggests that even the museum may be surpassed by the art catalog or book, in which all remaining vestiges of context—differences of size or of the texture of surfaces, for example—can be eliminated. The museum as a frame tends in the direction of Dada, that is, a pure structuralism in which each work of art refers only to itself and to every other work of art. The content of art—what art is about—is art; the context has been (almost) entirely "suspended."

Malraux tells us that the first picture frames represented window frames, so that the painting appeared as a window-view upon its content, taken to be a world (263). The frame established a finite place of "rendering" in which the play of light might be synthesized in the artist's interpretation or creative organization of a world (104). These pre-modern frames do not so much separate as connect content and context. Art represents something beyond itself; it links[2] man with the universe (602).

As art becomes modern, however, representation is dominated by the medium and by style, and "execution" replaces rendering (113, 116). Man becomes aware of a split in consciousness, between

---

[2] As T. E. Hulme says, it "adjusts" man's relationship with the universe. Hulme summarizes Wilhelm Worringer's theories, which are discussed further in Chapter Two.

the knowing subject and the known object; the existential copula, the possibility of true propositions and of self-identity, is thrown into question. The external world loses its reality and the artist himself replaces the traditional "subject" of painting (101). Art becomes an end in itself, a content without context.

The museum, as the modern frame, places works of art into juxtaposition with one another and suspends the question of context. It establishes an order, an arrangement in which the meaning of the work is not some possible reference to a reality beyond the work, but rather the content of the work in relation to the contents of other works of art, the transformations of an evolving, or a fixed, style. Corresponding to the art museum in the realm of literature is the library. The library is the modern literary frame par excellence.

No doubt we could carry a comparison of frames too far. It is tempting to compare the picture frame to the binding of a book. Both establish a context which is essential to the content, and yet which can be separated from that content. The painting remains the same on different frames, yet without a frame it is folded or wadded or rolled up. The book is the same in different bindings, but without a binding, its pages are disordered and lost. One difference, however, becomes apparent. There is only one *Las Meninas, and a* many copies of the original. But except for manuscript histories, we do not usually distinguish between one copy of a book and another; they are all "copies." This suggests that literature, as a content, is further removed from its context than is art.

Both the picture frame and the binding also establish a contextual space—a plane and a volume—which is filled by the content. This content, in turn, determines another space, a represented "world." We are at least partially aware of how context-determined space and content-determined space interact in the painting, but we tend to think that they are more or less irrelevant to one another in the case of literature. This difference is probably related to the one noted above, and again, context is further separated from content in literature.

We may question whether literary frames can ever connect context and content, as the frames of art at least once did and still do, if only in ambiguous ways—e.g., the interplay which Husserl and Foucault note. Must written words be totally separate from reality? Plato seems to suggest as much in the famous

Myth of Theuth, in the *Phaedrus*. Socrates describes writing as "a receipt [*pharmakon*] for recollection, not for memory," producing "the conceit of wisdom instead of real wisdom." The *pharmakon* will, he claims, cause people to "become forgetful" because writing replaces things with external signs.

> . . . once a thing is committed to writing it circulates equally among those who understand the subject and those who have no business with it . . . if it is ill-treated or unfairly abused it always needs its parent [the spoken word, dialectic] to come to its rescue; it is quite incapable of defending or helping itself. (96–97)

In contrast to this "shadow" writing[3], Socrates advocates "the kind that is written on the soul of the hearer together with understanding," which can properly participate in the dialectic, the way to the vision of the eternal. Writing, as "recollection," can only present a non-identical likeness, a simulacrum of the eternal.[4]

However, in this same passage (no. 275), Socrates claims that "writing involves a similar disadvantage to painting," which is also unable to answer questions addressed to it. The relation between written sign and idea is analogous to that between painted image and living soul. If they are analogous in their disconnection between content and context, are they not also analogous in their connection of the two?

We must not overlook the irony that Socrates's attack on the written word is presented in Plato's written text, and the possibility of duplicity here.[5] Socrates's words cannot "defend themselves" against the context which Plato gives them, or which I

---

3 Cf. *The Republic*, with its metaphoric structures of light and shadow.

4 See the *Symposium* (351).

5 Cf. Jacques Derrida's much noted discussion of Plato's double use of *pharmakon*, in *Dissemination*. See also 1979:121; 1976:292. According to Liddell and Scott's lexicon, *pharmakon* may be defined as: medicine (drug), poison (drug), potion (or spell), something producing (procuring) an effect. A study of various translations of the *Phaedrus* reveals how troublesome this word has been to translators. For a different approach to Plato's theory of writing, see Walter Ong, *The Presence of the Word*. Derrida's controversial questioning of Plato is in a way an inverting of Plato and consequent rejection of the reality of presence, a deconstruction* of Western metaphysics at its source. See Chapter Five. Also see the Seventh Letter frequently attributed to Plato, wherein the possibility of truth being found in writing is placed in question—and again, it is questioned in a written document.

have given them. This does not mean, however, that there is no connection between content and context, but rather that the ideal, perfect connection essential to what Socrates here calls "understanding" is disrupted by the written word. Writing creates the possibility (perhaps the necessity) of misunderstanding between the source and the recipient of knowledge, a slippage which must be "rescued" by, and would not be possible in, the spoken word, which is the presence of the one to the other. The spoken word lives; the written word is dead.

What Malraux called a suppression of reference in modern art may along these lines be re-conceived as a disruption of reference, which may be modern in that modern artists and writers are concerned with it—modern alienation is obsessed with it—but which is as old as art and literature are.

Even in the fantastic libraries of Jorge Luis Borges, the disconnection between context and content is not complete. Although God appears in "The Library of Babel" as a self-contained, circular book occupying a unique room to itself (and whose existence is doubtful), nonetheless there is the hope of "a book which is the cipher and compendium of *all the rest*" (85, emphasis Borges's), and the narrator concludes his account with the thesis that the Library's infinite periodicity "would constitute an order: Order itself" (88). In "The Secret Miracle," the major character, Jaromir Hladik, dreams (on the eve of his execution) of the Clementine Library, where he is told that "God is in one of the letters of one of the pages of one of the 400,000 volumes" (147). He touches a tiny letter on a map of India in a "useless" atlas; God grants his prayer for more time.

In these stories (and perhaps in all of Borges's stories), we see the same sort of infinite, self-referential exchange of context and content that we noted earlier in the two paintings, as understood by Husserl and Foucault. The dream changes reality; the library is in the book. Author, reader, and character alternate ambiguously with one another. At the "center" lies that disruption of understanding which Socrates identified with the written letter; the alphabet itself is a major "character" in both of the stories noted above. The result is not a complete separation of content and context but a radical upsetting of the distinction between the two and thus also of the self-identity of either. Neither "literature for literature's sake" nor "reality for reality's sake" are

possible, but this disturbance of their separation is also a disturbance of their connection, and it threatens the operation of the
frame.

3. Sense and Reference

In stories like those of Borges, and in paintings like those mentioned above, the frames which establish and are established by—
we need the verbal middle voice here—context and content
threaten to disappear. Such stories are what Robert Scholes has
called "anti-narratives." The improbability of any order appears,[6]
and an eruption of chaos seems imminent. How can this happen?

To answer these questions, we turn to Gottlob Frege's distinction between "sense" and "reference."[7] Frege notes that any
sign—"name, combination of words, letter" (57)—has not only a
reference (an object, using that word very generally as that to
which it points) but also a sense, which contains its "mode of
presentation." Thus "the reference of 'evening star' would be the
same as that of 'morning star,' but not the sense." The sense
mediates between the sign and the reference; a single reference
may be given many senses, and a single sense may be expressed
with various signs.

This distinction may be applied not only to the "names" of
objects, but also to sentences. (Frege hesitates to apply it to the
names of concepts or relations.) A sentence is composed of signs;
it contains a "thought"—which is its sense—and it may indicate
a reference. This reference is its truth-value; only if we consider
a sentence true does it have a reference (73).

The signs which express a sense—e.g., the words which tell a
story—would seem to belong to what I have above called the "context." They are not identical with the sense—other signs may
express the same sense—yet there is no sense without them. What
Frege calls the "reference" also belongs to the context, in that
when we ask whether a story (or painting, etc.) is true or not, we
seek to establish a congruity between content and context. For this
reason also, the content is what Frege calls "sense." An artistic or
literary work may have no context in that its reference is mistaken

6 See Foucault's discussion of Borges's "orders" (1970:xv–xvii).
7 In a revision of the translation of Frege's essay, *Bedeutung* has been translated as "meaning," not "reference." I retain the earlier English translation, as I
want to use "meaning" for both "sense" and "reference."

(not true) or because we refuse to consider its truth value ("art for art's sake," the Husserlian *epochē*,* etc.), but it must always have a context of a system of signs which "incarnate" it. We can imagine a story with sense but no reference (such as a myth that is no longer believed), but we cannot conceive of a story without sense.

Even "nonsense stories" and poems must have sense, in order to be at all perceived as story or poem. Lewis Carroll's "Jabberwocky," for example—disregarding Humpty Dumpty's exegesis of the poem in *Through the Looking Glass* as well as any private significance it may have had for the author—still must give the reader some vague sort of sense, a "sense of a sense," which makes it recognizable as "nonsense." Perhaps it is only the verse form and the identifiable words. We may find even less signifying material than that in a story in an unknown language, but some must be present for us to identify it as "a story in an unknown language." This is, again, the self-referentiality of the sign. At some point, signification ceases—would we know a hieroglyphic poem as such? Yet even hieroglyphics can be recognized—and at that point, sense (content) would also cease. There can be no story (painting, etc.) without sense—when we no longer know the writing to be writing.

Frege's distinction helps us to understand both the separability of content and context, and also their ultimate inseparability, as noted above. Although our interest here is not in specific techniques, we might expect to find three basic types of frames, corresponding to sign, sense, and reference, and all contributing to the integration of context and content. Sign-frames would include what an Aristotelian poetics called "diction," the appropriate language, and which would consist not only of the choice and interplay of words, but grammar, punctuation, etc., as well. Reference-frames would include at least some generic indicators (see Chapters Three and Four of this work); the possibility that some generic indicators—such as verse forms—are sign-frames suggests that sign and reference are not so far apart, as my use of the word "context" for both implies. Other framing techniques which might fit more than one category would be titles, footnotes, and introductions. Sense-frames would establish the narrative constituents—characters, events, settings, etc.—and would necessarily point in the "direction" of either the sign or the reference (see Chapter Two).

Because it must mediate sign and reference, sense must be
"divided" into its relations to each. Frege largely ignores the
relation of sense to sign and focuses almost entirely on the relation to reference; this is not without importance. However—
although he does not refer to Frege at all—Seymour Chatman
shows us how this double relation is possible. Chatman divides
"narrative structure" into four elements (22–24): "media in so far
as they can communicate . . ." (sign systems), "representations of
objects and actions in real and imagined worlds that can be
imitated . . ." (reference), "narrative discourse," and "narrative
story components." The last two—what the Russian formalist
theorists called the "plot" (*sjužet*)* and the "fable" (*fabula*),*
respectively—both appear to be aspects of sense or content;
Chatman identifies them as "expression form" and "content
form."[8] Superimposing terminologies, the following table of
"equivalencies" results:[9]

CONTEXT	CONTENT	CONTEXT
SIGN	SENSE	REFERENCE
MEDIA	PLOT FABLE	REPRESENTATIONS

TABLE 1

The plot (or discourse) of a narrative—the actual arrangement
of words and presentation of story—is the sense as it relates to
the signs; this is where the structuralist distinction between
langue, or "competence," and *parole*, or "performance," comes
into play. The fable—what "actually happened" in reality or
fantasy—is the sense related to the reference.

This distinction helps us to explore further the inter-relations

---

[8] The first two are the "expression substance" and "content substance";
whether our disagreement over the word "content" is important I will not consider here. I use the terms "fable" and "plot" rather than "story" and "discourse"
at this point, because I do not want to prejudice the word "story."

[9] We must be very cautious in passing between these equivalencies, as well as
the ones in Table 2. The tables suggest a translatability between different theories which is filled with important and dangerous possibilities. Although I do not
here give a chapter to the problem of translation, it will reappear at several
points in this work.

of content and context. As Frege states, "a truth value is the reference of a sentence having a thought as its sense" (78).[10] This "thought" is clearly the fable; the plot would be the syntagm or word sequence. Given a truth value, the thought must be affirmed or denied; it becomes a matter of belief (in a wide sense of that word). To suspend belief—if that is possible—is to withhold a truth value, to refuse to move from sense to reference, and therefore to separate content from context. Hermeneutical and literary theories (such as Gerald Graff's) which insist that literature must be discussed and judged at least in terms of its propositional content must deny the possibility of such a suspension—of a content which can be separated from its context—or they may permit a suspension only within the framework of a "larger" (and therefore less obvious) belief, hidden assumptions which inevitably integrate the content into a context.

On the other hand, those who would permit a suspension of belief—including structuralist and phenomenological theorists, as well as the somewhat older "New Critics" and numerous others, back as far as Coleridge and Kant—would claim that a separation of content from context—a reduction—is not only possible but necessary for a proper understanding of the work of art or literature. I stand among this group—or cluster of groups—and yet I am not entirely satisfied with these claims. This book is written to explore and criticize the metaphysics implicit in both "propositional" and "anti-propositional" approaches, and to argue that neither is therefore capable of reaching the limits of story. Further consideration of the problem of belief will be presented in Chapter Three.

Another contribution of the distinction between plot and fable is clarification of the controversial matter of translation. If we consider the sense of a literary work as its fable, intending as its reference the representation of an objective world, then it is certainly and accurately translatable. According to Frege, the sense (or thought) must be distinguished from the subjective ideas of reader and author, which are untranslatable—i.e., they can never be adequately communicated. Many different senses,

---

[10] The relation between sentences and stories is a very complex one, and it will be further explored in Chapters Three and Five, along with Frege's theory of "concepts." Cf. Calloud: 25; Detweiler: 113. For the present considerations, no distinction seems necessary.

however, can present an identical reference, and therefore these senses are logically equivalent; they translate into one another. Chatman calls this "reading out." On the other hand, if we consider the sense as the plot, which leads us back to the system of signs (paradigm) or medium of the work, then it is untranslatable. Translation involves a change of medium and/or signifiers and an inevitable transformation of the plot.

> . . . here belong also the colouring and shading which poetic eloquence seeks to give to the sense. Such colouring and shading are not objective, and must be evoked by each hearer or reader according to the hints of the poet or the speaker. (Frege: 61)

Insofar as these "hints" occur in the signs, as they must in any written text, a change of signs brings a discontinuity in translation.

This prospect of untranslatability reflects the "imperfection" of language which troubles Frege. He claims that all sentences presuppose reference; they all intend a truth value. This is also the claim which Graff makes, as noted above, and is opposed to the position of New Critics such as I. A. Richards, which is that poetic language—as opposed to scientific language—uses referential statements only as the vehicle for non-referential purposes. The poet is not making claims about something, but rather expressing his/her feelings about something. Frege and Graff, however, assert that feelings must be grounded in belief, and therefore statements of feeling imply assertions about beliefs (Frege: 67). However, Frege notes a problem: ". . . languages have the fault of containing expressions which fail to designate an object . . . because the truth of some sentence is a prerequisite" (69). If the truth of that sentence is unknown, or if its truth is dependent in turn on the truth of yet another sentence, and so on, then the original sentence, although grammatically proper, may have an indeterminate reference. Even mathematical language, Frege notes, is imperfect, because an arrangement of signs may represent a divergent infinite series.*

> A logically perfect language (*Begriffsschrift*) should satisfy the conditions, that every expression grammatically well constructed as a proper name out of signs already introduced shall in fact designate an object, and that no new sign shall be introduced as a proper name without being secured a reference. (70)

Kurt Gödel's incompleteness theorems, furthermore, imply that a language, as a logical system, must be incomplete or inconsistent. In other words, there must always be some "expression" within the language which cannot be accounted for by the system of the language itself, a fault or imperfection at which the language as an intelligible whole breaks down. This incompleteness, or non-identity, becomes apparent at that point where language seeks to refer to itself.[11]

Frege's example of the imperfection of language is a metaphor*: "The will of the people." I shall argue in Chapter Five that all metaphors are "divergent infinite series," and that the fundamental metaphoricity of language (and therefore of story) as writing disrupts and is concealed within the metaphysics of the limits of story.

Jacques Maritain claims that the principle of identity is fundamental to metaphysics; it adds determination, or "essential quality," as a predicate to the subject, which is posited as existing (92). In the passage cited at the opening of this chapter, Husserl is concerned with the problem of the identity of the noematic content. Frege begins his essay with considerations of identity. "a = a" and "a = b" (assuming that the latter is true) refer to the same object, yet they differ in "mode of presentation" (sense) because the signs differ. These differences of presentation permit the identity to be more than a tautology, and thus to contain "actual knowledge" (57). Yet this metaphysical identity is founded upon metaphor, the coincident difference and identity of the sign, and the fundamental imperfection of language. There is a non-identity at the heart of identity, which suggests a chaos at the center of reason.

This non-identity or chaos cannot be said or thought, because that would turn it into sense, that which it is not. For language to make sense, it must presuppose the principle of identity, and to speak of chaos is self-contradictory. Language establishes an order and thereby a world, as we shall argue in Chapter Two; chaos undoes world. Thus at the borders of metaphysics, we arrive at an ineffability and must turn with the

---

[11] Gödel develops his theorems with respect to the "language" of Russell and Whitehead's *Principia Mathematica*, but he explicitly states that they apply as well to any language which is "ω-consistent" (596). We are again faced with a dangerous translation, this time between the "artificial" number systems which Gödel was considering and "natural" languages.

mystics to a sort of negative theology. This theology would also be a self-contradiction, insofar as we define "theology" as answering a specific set of questions (about God, etc.) or fulfilling a religious function—in other words, as long as we see theology as a meaningful system. If we "see" theology at all, it has unity and sense; it is metaphysical. This negative theology must then be non-sense; it must be unintentional and ungraspable, violated and destroyed by meaning. To conceive of it would be to lose it; it must rather conceive—or de-conceive—itself upon us. It must be accepted as a vague, invisible discomfort, a threat to the traditional metaphysics of theology, a sort of theological anti-matter. It may provide a tension from which new theologies can be generated. It cannot be dismissed as a modern breakdown of structure or loss of faith. This theology of chaos will never appear in this or any other book. All that can be achieved is an infinite series of approximations to it, which may point the way to the source of language itself.

Where are these borders of metaphysics? One border lies within the sign. Husserl distinguishes between the material phase—"sensile *hylē*"*—and the noesis* or noetic phase—"intentional *morphē*" as the "duality and unity" which constitute experience (226). "The stream of phenomenological being has a twofold bed: a material and a noetic" (230). The noetic includes the sign intended as a signifying object—the sign as a sign. The hyletic includes the sign considered as pre-signifying or pre-hermeneutical—"the opaqueness of a body" (Derrida, 1973:38) which is not yet a sign, that which we intend as a sign. For example, it is the actual ink on paper, artificially separated from the significance which we intend for it, even the minimal significance of it as a "word." The hyletic thus cannot be said or thought; it must forever be overlooked and abandoned by intentionality. It is the materiality of written language which necessarily distorts the intended meaning.[12] The story, or the meaningful text, must continually "forget" this meaningless material, this non-metaphysical "trace" (Derrida, 1973:127, note). Yet without it, there is no sign. This is the non-identity within the sign which troubles Frege's account of sense and to which Socrates's attack on the written

[12] Derrida speaks of this as the *étron*, or waste matter, which is essential to the "life" of the word but immediately eliminated in the search for meaning (1979:161ff.). See also Derrida, 1973, *passim.*

word is directed; it is this which causes the need of the noetic form to be "rescued" by its originating intention. Its non-identity, or self-referentiality, must be cancelled in order for it to produce sense and reference. That which gives recollection is itself beyond recollection.

If the sign as non-identical contains a noetic limit of metaphysics, then we may expect the reference also to be non-identical, and to contain a noematic limit. Chatman (drawing upon Booth) again provides us with a way to understand this. Narrative, as fable/plot, lies along an exchange or tension between an "implied author"* or "official scribe"—an implied version of the "real author," present in the narrative (148)—and an "implied reader"*—the counterpart of the implied author, also present in the narrative (150). Although these may actually appear as characters in some narratives, they are perhaps more commonly found in the background, as the horizon against which the events and objects of the narrative appear.

The hermeneutical exchange or circle which constitutes the narrative, between author and reader, is therefore also fractured by the non-identity of the real and the implied. Although the implied author and reader do not comprise the entirety of the representation (reference), they are the poles between which representation becomes possible. They are the "truth-value" of the story. Therefore, this non-identity is not that of the hyletic and the noetic, which belong to the intentional act of consciousness, but it is rather within the intended meaning of consciousness (the noema, in Husserl's terminology). It corresponds to Husserl's distinction between the "real" and the "immanent" (237ff.), the essence which remains after the question of reality has been "bracketed" or suspended. The immanent is "irreal"; it cannot be said that it actually exists. For example, the real would include my actual existence as a conscious being (a being-conscious of something), and the immanent would be that which remains if I reflectively suspend the question (or the unreflective assumption) of reality and ask, "Who or what am I, as a consciousness? What is the content of this consciousness that is 'I'?" Similarly, the implied reader (or author) arises as a reflective tension between the narrative and the real reader (or author). This tension centers upon the problems of propositional content and belief. We may now supplement Table 1 as follows:

CONTEXT	CONTENT	CONTEXT
SIGN	SENSE	REFERENCE
MEDIA	PLOT FABLE	REPRESENTATIONS
NOESIS	(CONTENT)	NOEMA
HYLE MORPHE		IMMANENT REAL

TABLE 2

The distinction between author and reader (real or implied) does not cause a problem here, for as I noted earlier, certain works of art and literature establish an infinite interplay between author, reader, and characters (painter, spectator, and subject) which short-circuits this distinction, or rather, which must be overcome if such a distinction is to be established. This distinction, then, emerges from the reference-frames of the narrative— the suppression of the non-identity which I am considering here—and must not be presupposed. Thus we may say that what lies "outside" of this boundary is the "beholder," whom I mentioned in the first part of this chapter, and who is neither author nor reader nor the "real world" in general, and yet is all three. A number of philosophers have pointed in the direction of this beholder—for example, Bergson's intuited duration, and Heidegger's "opening" in which Being appears—which grounds and lies outside of ("at the end of") metaphysics and which is necessarily forgotten by the "false metaphysics" of the European tradition and by what Heidegger calls "technology." We cannot enter this discussion here, except to note with these thinkers that the "beholder," as used here, is not a person or indeed any sort of determined consciousness, but rather that which makes conceptual and other determinations possible. It is, according to Fragment I of Parmenides, "the unshaken heart of well-rounded truth."[13] This image of the metaphysical sphere, with the beholder at its center, is a crucial one. Is it possible that the hyletic phase of the sign and the real beholder, at the metaphysical limits of the context, are one? Can the non-identity within

---

[13] Heidegger's controversial translation has "the untrembling heart of unconcealment, well-rounded" (1972:67). The ambiguous reference of "well-rounded" is crucial. Cf. Derrida, 1981:163–64; Bachelard, 1964:234.

the sign and that within reference be identical? Whatever
exceeds these limits is necessarily unspeakable; therefore no significant distinction can be made, nor can an identity be asserted.
The hyletic materiality of the sign and the real beholder "are"
non-identical and non-different.

4. Frames, Value, and Canon

Therefore the realm of metaphysics lies within two limits,
which may be identically non-identical, and which we have
approached in the pre-hermeneutical, hyletic phase of the sign
on the one hand, and the real beholder, on the other. Because
these limits cannot be spoken—except perhaps by the poet or
the mystic, and then only metaphorically, i.e., inaccurately, non-
identically—they are also the limits of language and must also
be limits of story, if we understand that story depends upon
language. Frames, as the connection and separation of context
and content, are the tissue or glue which holds this metaphysical
realm together, and therefore the frame establishes the story as
what it is, as an identity, by suppressing the non-identity which
is enfolded within metaphysics, and yet without which there is
no metaphysics. The stories (and art works) which confuse content and context in an infinite regression/reversal of self-
referentiality seek to "break" the frames and to de-construct
metaphysics by disrupting the identity of the work. To the
extent that these stories succeed in breaking their frames, they
become senseless and cease to be stories. This is precisely what
we find happening in paradoxical works such as those of Borges.
The frames suppress this disruption and establish the identity of
the story. The framed story is a world, and the framed world—
such as Husserl's recollection of his visit to the gallery—is a
story. Without the frame there is neither story nor world. We
shall see in greater detail how this happens in the next four
chapters.

In establishing the story as what it is, the frame gives it a
value, which may be understood morally, aesthetically, and
socio-economically. Its identity establishes its worth, as what it
may be exchanged for, what it is equivalent to. We noted earlier
a frame which establishes the worth of a painting but does not
apply to literary works: its status as an original. (Original manu-
scripts are worth more than common paperback editions, but

recognition

this relates to their worth as historical objects, not as stories.)
Related to this is value as possession. The owner and the owned
"possess" one another and give value to each other. The value of
a story may be its author's intent or its reader's response; both
are forms of ownership. The author is the "original owner" of
the story; the reader makes it "his own" when he or she understands it as "authentic."

Another, also related, measure of worth is popularity, or to
speak more generally, a sort of socio-economic "recognition."
That which is totally unrecognized is worthless and ceases to
have identity; it loses its metaphysical status. Of course, the
category of "garbage" still entails a sort of recognition, but it is
defined less in terms of its own frames—the trash can, the city
dump—than by its exclusion from all other frames. Yet it still
remains within the limits of metaphysics, which we recognize by
"saving" it, if it may be potentially valuable within some
presently-unknown frame, other than its original purpose. Nonetheless, garbage remains near the borders of metaphysics, and
some of it is doubtless continually "drifting off" beyond those
borders.

The worth of something is also its use, its practical value. use
Thus fiction is sometimes distinguished from fact as that which
is useless—"pretending" vs. "the real thing." Truth-value, which
modern science grants only to fact and to generalizations about
facts, is also a value. Fictional works here appear very similar to
garbage; a highly technological civilization does not know what
to do with them. A common response to this situation has been
to assign to "impractical" literature and art a separate kind of
value—in effect, a separate metaphysical realm—from that of
science and technology: the value of feelings, of emotions, or of
style. The library and the museum segregate literature and art
from "real life," just as the city dump segregates garbage. The
thrust of Graff's attacks on much modern literary theory is that
many theorists are contributing to this segregation, rather than
fighting it.

However, not all value consists in ownership, recognition, or
usefulness. It is sometimes claimed that the "greatness" of a work
of literature or art is none of these, but something else, over
which we have no control. In fact, the work may have lain long
unrecognized (although "saved"), its author unknown, and it
may be impractical to us, like the cave paintings in France.

Richards, at the opposite extreme from Graff, insists on the ultimacy of poetry's emotive meaning, its ability to augment a coherency or completeness of the self. Northrop Frye, in his arguments for the mythic function of narrative, makes very similar claims. It is precisely the "worthlessness" of literary art which gives it its greatest value: it can transcend all our partial interests—our modern alienations—and integrate them into a greater whole. That which is the source of all value cannot itself have a value. Despite the obvious oppositions, Frye and Richards, like Graff, seek an integration of poetry and reality.

Yet Graff wants poetry to be rationally explicable—"propositional"—and his opponents claim that it is fundamentally irrational. Poetry does not so much "say" as "express" reality; it does not so much describe as prescribe (or create) it. This irrationality, however, is not the irrationality of the non-metaphysical, of which no account may be given. Rather, this irrationality is rationally accountable; we can explain the why and how, and describe the objects and circumstances, of feelings of anger, lust, etc. To do so presupposes a metaphysical framework: that of psychoanalysis, behaviorism, Marxism, etc. The disagreement between Graff and his opponents is over the priority of the conscious ("rational," ideological) and the non-conscious (emotive); it is a disagreement about metaphysical frames, which can only be resolved in terms of one such metaphysics or another.

Identity as value, as a question of subjectivity—of the individual or the social group—is established in relation to the metaphysical limit of reference. In the "opposite" direction—the limit of the sign—identity is established as the question of canon, the selection of texts, as objectivities. To pick up a book and begin to read it—or to turn toward one painting or speaker, and away from another—is already to assign to it a significance. Not to read is to consign it to insignificance, or at best only potential significance. Here something very similar to what I said above about garbage and the worthless is operating. However, if we confine value to the range of the subjective, then canon concerns the objective structure of texts, their generation and articulation in particular ways. Here too there are questions of conscious and non-conscious "motivation" and causality. Again we note that as we approach either limit, the "opposites" of canon and value seem to be merging. Thus the structuralists, who are especially concerned with canon, are pushed inexorably toward exegesis—a question of value—and the exegetes cannot ignore structure. For example, Stanley Hauerwas, who develops ethical theory in relation to the concept of story, must establish a meta-ethical* criterion in terms of which some stories are better than others—a criterion of canon. Canon and value are the two sides of the meaning of the story—its identity— which is established by metaphysical frames.

The byword of a great deal of modern criticism—"to return to the text"—conceals a great deal of metaphysics, by presuming that the text "is" there, an identical, neutral thing, which we can turn to at will. It makes the will (choice) of the critic dependent upon the text as a thing by itself, rather than that which creates the text by choosing it. If Graff and Fry choose the "same" text, it is not the same text. We cannot return to the text because the very (metaphoric) "act of turning" establishes the text as a meta-physical entity. This is the "noetic bed" of "phenomenological being." This paradox has been marvelously developed by Borges in his story, "Pierre Menard, Author of Don Quixote." Menard, a twentieth-century writer, seeks to reproduce the *Don Quixote*— not a modern version, but the "same" text as that of Cervantes, writing in the seventeenth century. "The text of Cervantes and that of Menard are verbally identical, but the second is almost infinitely richer" (52). However, "the archaic style of Me-nard . . . suffers from a certain affectation. Not so that of his precursor . . ." (53). A text from Isaiah is not the same in the words of Jesus as in those of the prophet; it cannot be the same, unless we assume an identical intentionality, in which case Jesus is Isaiah (and Menard is Cervantes). But if this is so, how can we ever discuss the "same" text, the "same" ideas, or anything else?

What makes one text the "same" as another? If you and I have two copies of the same edition of the same book, then the noetic phase (from the shape of the binding down to the number of "typos") is identical, although the actual material substance, the hyletic, is different. If we have two different editions of the book, there will be formal as well as material differences. What if we have the same book in two different languages, or two different translations of it in the same language? The Gospel of John in English is in some respects "more different" from the Greek text than it is from the Gospel of Luke in English. Yet we are inclined to say that the two "Johns" are in some important ways the same, and that both are different from Luke in any language. We are also inclined to say that one translation of a

context

work is better than another; we are very close to value here. All of these claims have both intellectual and affective components, and all are possible only by presuming that the text has an identity. The alternative is that your book and mine are not the same, even if the edition is (formally) identical. Of course we can draw a line somewhere in between these positions—a "standard" edition, an "authorized" translation, etc.—but this also presupposes a metaphysics on which we base our choice and thereby form the text. No amount of close textual study can resolve the issue apart from metaphysics.

The frame establishes the identity of the story, what it is, by establishing a value and a canonical text. These are not two separate acts, but the one act of framing. As Heidegger says, Framing (capitalized in the English translation) stands between Being and Appropriation (1972:53). It makes the non-metaphysical into the metaphysical by appropriating it, by making it our own. I argue that this involves a suppression of the chaotic, that which can never be said and therefore can never be ours. The frame defines the fundamental incompleteness or incoherence within the story as unimportant and irrelevant—i.e., as garbage—and authorizes its "elimination." Because the frame establishes the identity of the story, it is metaphysical.

I have not yet defined "story," nor will I do so here. If the question of metaphysics is before all else the question of identity, then story may only be defined upon the completion of a critique of its metaphysics. But how can we begin this critique if we don't know what story is? Already we are caught in a hermeneutical circle. In order to start, we make a choice, establish a frame. "Story" becomes a word in terms of which we define other words. Does this choice not establish a metaphysics, which will inevitably entangle our critique? Like language itself, this critique—and therefore also our definition of story—must be incomplete. Like every metaphysics, it will have its faults, fracture-lines along which it can be de-constructed with a judicious blow. We cannot establish all the limits of story, only some of them—and then only from within the metaphysical realm. Many important questions will be omitted or given only slight consideration here; I apologize for this and invite the reader to further the critique in those areas. What I do attempt in this book is a series of approximations to some central questions which must be answered by anyone wishing to explore what story is, or to use the concept of story in the service of some other end.

Chapter Two
FORM AND WORLD

The framed story is a world, and the framed world is a story. The world as humans experience it is found within—it "occupies," it "possesses"—temporal duration and the three dimensions of space. Time and space are the fundamental forms of our perception of external objects, as Kant pointed out. The problem of form becomes a bit more complex if we consider "internal" (psychic) objects, such as dreams, and it appears to change substantially if we turn to ideal objects, such as mathematical formulas, which are not "real," but will always be true. What about stories? Although we defer a full consideration of the referentiality of story to Chapter Three, we can already note that stories relate to space and time on two different "levels." There is the space and time of the telling/hearing or writing/ reading of the signs of which it is composed. There is the space and time of the objects and events which are found in the story—the world without and the world within, or as stated in Chapter One, context and content.

If we consider story as an act of transmission or communication, a narrative, then these two levels are the narration and the narrated. Neither the space nor the time of the narrated need be (or often is) identical with that of the narration. However, as we noted earlier, the metaphysics of frames unites these levels, establishing an identity, which is the story. Thus we must expect the identity of the story to "control" its spatial and temporal forms, and that they will in turn play a part in its metaphysics.

1. Temporal Form

Perhaps the fundamental assertion of temporal form in literary theory is Aristotle's claim that in tragedy and epic—and by extension in all stories—the plot, the central ingredient of the story, must center around action, and action takes place in time.

This is why plot must have a beginning, a middle, and an end: it must "come from" a specific origin, at a specific point in time, and "go to" a coherent conclusion, also at a specific point in time; otherwise it loses its unity and becomes aimless, chaotic (1450a–b). Meaning is found in ordered time, and without this plotted unity of action, there can be no meaning. Plot is, as Northrop Frye has noted, the *mythos* or narrative as the rationally communicable sense of the story. This sense is found, at least in part, in the ordering of the temporal structure.

Aristotle is evidently talking about the narrated content of story, what it is about. Almost all of the extant *Poetics*, as the title implies, is about how stories are made, or ought to be made. Stories seek to imitate reality, according to Aristotle—meaning things as they are or should be—and reality is ultimately teleological, movement toward a goal (cf. Ricoeur, 1980:174). Aristotle is also concerned with the context of the story, insofar as it has an effect on its audience. The catharsis of the story arises from its reference to the reality of the spectator's lives and the release of emotion that occurs at specific points in the temporal unfolding of the plot is prescribed by the plot's development through complication, climax, and denouement (1455b–56b). The temporal order of the plot reflects the ability of the spectators to remember it. The temporality of the narrated depends upon the temporality of narration.

This temporality of story belongs to linear time. It does not repeat or reverse upon itself. Although Aristotle allows the epic poem to relate in sequence events that "actually" occur simultaneously—e.g., Telemachos seeking his father while Odysseus struggles homeward—the tragic drama must follow rigid chronological order. Any deviation from linearity weakens the order, and hence the unity, the identity, of story.

Modifications to the theory which explain and permit flashbacks and flashforwards, the slowing down or speeding up of narrative time, etc., have not substantially altered this notion of story as built around a linear order of time. In the eighteenth century, Lessing responded to theories which originated with Horace and Simonides and which sought a common basis of the two arts by distinguishing between painting and poetry as the arts appropriate to space and time, respectively, reinforcing the Aristotelian theory. Lessing also stressed that the form of the content depends upon "the conditions of human perception"

(Frank, 1963:8). The visual art must be spatial, and the aural one must be temporal.

Contemporary theorists—even those who have raised fundamental questions about the theory of temporal form—continue to view temporality as the basic form of narrative, a form which may admit of deviations, but which—because they are deviations—is never entirely suspended.

The theory has a theological dimension often overlooked by literary theorists. Although I am not here asserting any causal relationship between the theological and literary dimensions of the theory, the congruence between them is important. Theologians of the Judeo-Christian tradition have stressed the importance to both religions of history—i.e., of linear temporality. Temporality is seen as fundamental to both the content of that tradition—the world created by God and moving inexorably under God's "authorship" toward its end—and to its context—the believer (as individual and as community) in relation to God. Only in such a framework are theological concepts such as justice, grace, covenant, election, salvation, etc. commonly discussed. Thus "story" is almost inevitably discussed as "history" (linear time).

As a result, there have been a number of attempts to apply narrative theory to theology, in relation to temporal form. For example, faith has been defined as

> an impassioned, tacit groping toward intimations of truth not yet realized or incompletely disclosed . . . in the hope of ultimately participating in the realization or disclosure of the truth in question. (Cannon: 562)

The movement toward discovery implicit in this definition (influenced by the thought of Polanyi) is also an aspect of Aristotle's theory, namely, that plot moves toward denouement, which serves as the revelation of narrated "discovery" and the release of narrational catharsis. Stanley Hauerwas and Richard Bondi, speaking of theological ethics, claim that "we are forced to tell stories in order to capture our past, sustain our present, and give our future direction" (104). They focus upon character (another Aristotelian story-element, dependent upon the plot), and they see character as determined by memory as "presence":

> Memory has creative force when it reminds us not of past events but of the characters which produced them,

> and when the memory of that character challenges us to
> renounce it or be true to it in the present moment. (106)

Again, temporal unity is primary. In fact, it is characteristic of almost all of the contemporary theological studies of story to assume or assert the linear temporality of story.[1]

The fundamentally temporal form of biblical narrative is also widely accepted. The Bible is viewed as representing a history which proceeds in a linear manner from an unrepeatable act of creation through various hardships and triumphs (for both God and humans) to a final moment in which all temporal events will be completed. Outside of this procession there is no time—only, perhaps, the eternal—but within it, temporal order rules even over God, who is therefore regarded as the "God of history," and who is "present in history."

This notion of linear time and of temporal form, however, presents us with certain problems. These problems, first described by the ancient philosopher Zeno in his famous paradoxes, concern the attempt to conceive time as analogous to a line in space, where each moment or instant corresponds to a point on the line, and they demonstrate the impossibility of understanding movement—or identity in time—if time is so conceived. (Theologically, this is expressed as the "mystery" of God being eternal and yet immanent in history.) Henri Bergson, one of the two great modern philosophers of time, argued that the attempt to conceptualize duration leads to a "false metaphysics" of time, time treated as a mechanical, technical tool rather than as the living consciousness apart from which it does not exist. Duration cannot be conceived, but only intuited (1955:21–24).

> . . . imagine an infinitely small elastic body, contracted, if
> it were possible, to a mathematical point. Let this be
> drawn out gradually in such a manner that from the point
> comes a constantly lengthening line. . . . Let us bear in
> mind that this action [of tracing the line by drawing out
> the point], in spite of its duration, is indivisible if accom-
> plished without stopping, that if a stopping-point is in-
> serted, we have two actions instead of one, that each of
> these separate actions is then the indivisible operation of

---

[1] E.g., John S. Dunne, *A Search for God in Time and Memory*; Emil Facken-heim, *God's Presence in History*. These two excellent books are both very sensitive to narrative qualities in theology; both rely profoundly upon the notion of temporal form.

which we speak, and that it is not the moving action itself
which is divisible, but, rather, the stationary line it leaves
behind it as its track in space (26–27). . . . pure duration . . . excludes all idea of juxtaposition, reciprocal ex-
ternality, and extension. (26)

The conceptualizing of time ignores the unity-in-multiplicity
of duration, its interpenetration, without which the phenomenon
of memory is reduced to mechanical repetition and evolving life
is replaced with a clock-work mechanism. Consciousness is an
"inner duration," prolonging the past into the present: "Without
this survival of the past into the present there would be no duration, but only instantaneity" (40). Duration is the principle of
continuity in change, allowing the future to "unroll" into the
present and to be "rolled up" into the past (25–26), an identity
within movement which is deformed by "relative knowledge"
into the world of external, spatial relations between conceptualized "things." Bergson argues that the extremes of duration are
its total concentration in "an eternity of life" and its total atten-
uation or dispersion in "bare materiality." "Between these two
extreme limits intuition moves, and this movement is the very
essence of metaphysics" (49). This image of movement between
a center (intuited life as duration) and a circumference (conceptualized objects in material space) is a very important one. In
his essay on "Laughter," he applies these distinctions to literature
in the form of comedy: the essence of the comic is the encrusta-
tion of the mechanical—e.g., clock-work movements—upon the
living (the self, duration).

The other great modern philosopher of time, Martin Heidegger, also attacks the notion of linear time, and in a very similar way. "Real time," according to Heidegger, does not belong to
technology, the realm of "calculation," but it is instead the unity
of "presencing," in which Being simultaneously gives itself and
withdraws (reveals and hides itself).

> How are we to determine this giving of presencing that
> prevails in the present, in the past, in the future? Does this
> giving lie in this, that it reaches us, or does it reach us
> because it is in itself a reaching? The latter. Approaching,
> being not yet present, at the same time gives and brings
> about what is no longer present, the past, and conversely
> what has been offers future to itself. The reciprocal rela-
> tion of both at the same time gives and brings about the
> present (1972:13). . . . prior to all calculation of time and

> independent of such calculation, what is germane to the
> time-space of true time consists in the mutual reaching out
> and opening up of future, past and present. (14)

Time is pre-spatial and therefore pre-metaphysical, pre-
philosophical (16). It is the realm of "destiny" or "fate," which
corresponds closely with Bergson's notion of concentration. Both
Heidegger and Bergson explicitly reject the Kantian analysis of
time (as a perceptual form) as a linear sequence, and both question the value for knowledge of a representation based upon a
segmentation of the object of consciousness. Nonetheless, both
Heidegger and Bergson themselves use highly spatial images—
concentration vs. dispersion, the interplay of the four temporal
"dimensions"—in their discussions of time, moving however
towards the suggestion of a multi-dimensionality or manifold of
time and away from the notion of linearity.

John Vernon uses a Heideggerian analysis[2] of time as an
approach to modern literature, arguing that modern writers
either seek the fragmentation of linear, "spatialized time" into a
dissociated schizophrenia, or else they seek to overcome this
fragmentation in the integrated interplay of Heideggerian "real
time." Thus modern literature polarizes into something ap-
proaching, on the one hand, the purely spatial form of a map,
and on the other, the integral real time of a garden.

> A map . . . relates the whole to its parts as an addition of
> discrete entities rather than as a fluid unity of transfor-
> mations. The image of the map and of its counterpart,
> the labyrinth . . . is an image, John Barth points out, of
> exhaustion, of Western thought structures that have lost
> their cohesive force. . . . The definition of a map would
> obviously be destroyed if its parts could penetrate each
> other. Each area of a map is confined in its location. . . .
> Areas on a map are related only at their respective
> borders, so that no location can exist in itself and in any
> other location simultaneously. (10–11)

The map is the realm of logic, science, private property, and the
alienation of the subject: the realm of representation. Union of

---

[2] For another statement of a Heideggerian approach to narrative form, see
Paul Ricoeur, "Narrative Time." Ricoeur speaks of the episodic (linear
sequence) and the configurational (spatial form) as two elements of a dialectic
which forms the narrative, and as a case of Heideggerian historicality.

the different is only possible in map-space as juxtaposition or "mergence."*

In contrast, the garden is the realm of primal wholeness, fluidity, and unity in multiplicity. Time in the garden is not linear-spatial, but it is the time of the three "exstases" described by Heidegger:

> . . . the future and the past are both always opening and always closing; each shifts and transforms with the movement of time, and falling is both a falling into and out of itself. Falling [as the present] is always a momentum, and it gathers itself; but because it also loses itself, the expression of that momentum is in the future as well as in the past . . . that action in which the future pours into the past and swells it—and that action in which the past pours into the future and swells it. (138)

Falling is an act that is not only a fall but also a rising (139). The present is never strictly present—as a discrete object—but always also not present, withheld in the past or withdrawn into the future (Heidegger, 1972:22). It therefore "belongs" also to the past and the future; there are no boundaries between temporal moments. The garden integrates all temporal and spatial oppositions, including its own opposition to the map, by transforming them into an "organic" unity, a living identity. Thus the garden can unite with the map, but the map must oppose itself to the garden.

Vernon presents a strong argument for not only the existence but also the critical preferability of this literature of the garden (he cites as examples the works of James Dickey and Theodore Roethke). However, is he speaking of what we have called the narration or the narrated?

> My purpose in this work is . . . to uncover the world of a work of literature, or . . . of a school of literature, according to its own inner structural coordinates. Only in this manner can we apprehend the underlying structures of the culture from which that literature is inseparable. (xv)

What he calls "map space" remains in Vernon's methodology, as the work (narrated content) is seen to mirror the cultural world (narrational context). Despite his suggestive critique of spatialized time, we appear to remain in the realm of linear history. This difficulty also—and crucially—appears in his central metaphor for the alternative to that map space, the pre-Fallen Garden of Eden, which we will consider further in the final two parts of this chapter.

2. Spatial Form

The alternative to the garden type of narrative, in Vernon's view, is the narrative dominated by map space, in the modern extremes of which the linear sequence is fragmented and becomes labyrinthine. A multi-dimensional and potentially self-referential* spatiality "explodes" from within the confines of linearity. As Vernon recognizes, it is this literature which has been described by Joseph Frank in his controversial theory of spatial form.

Frank claims that spatiality tends to dominate the essential linear temporality of narrative in at least some stories. We should note that this is not a reference to the story's environment, setting, location, etc., which are in the Aristotelian scheme subservient to plot—i.e. to time. These elements of the narrated should not be ignored, however; Gaston Bachelard has described the considerable metaphysical importance of such spaces. An example of the relation between spatial elements and the spatial form of narrative will be considered below. Nonetheless, Frank's claim is that the form or structure of the story is spatially organized, that although we necessarily read or hear it sequentially (temporally), the story does not consist of an action but of a group of images or perspectives which we must juggle simultaneously, or juxtapose (in the manner of a collage or a multiple-exposure photograph).

Frank notes Lessing's distinction between spatial and temporal forms, and he claims that modern literature, in some important instances, has tended to reverse Lessing's thesis by striving for a spatial form, and that this change reflects a change in the "spiritual attitudes" of modern humanity (1963:53ff.). That such a reversal is possible, however, indicates a fundamental spatiality of all language and all literature, made particularly evident in these modern instances (1978:289–90).

Modern literature, according to Frank, is composed of isolated images or scenes, for which the flow of time is suspended or ignored.

> [A]ttention is fixed on the interplay of relationships within the immobilized time-area. These relationships

are juxtaposed independently of the progress of the narrative, and the full significance of the scene is given only by the reflexive relations among the units of meaning. (1963:15)

As far as I can tell, Frank's notion of the reflexive "space-logic" required by these narratives, violating the "normal" flow of linear temporality, is very close to the notion of self-referentiality developed in Chapter One. The effect of this spatiality in the story is not a denial of time, but rather, as in the works of Proust or Joyce, the transcendence of time, the creation of "eternal" meaning.

Frank attributes spatial form in literature, following Wilhelm Worringer's analyses of naturalism in art,[3] to modern humanity's disequilibrium with the universe. He is thus methodologically in agreement with Vernon, Lessing, and Aristotle, on the relation of narrated and narration. When people are in harmony with the world, art expresses their acceptance of the world in naturalistic forms, which in literature would stress temporality (this is Aristotle's and Lessing's point). When people are alienated from the world, art takes on non-naturalistic forms ("primitive," Byzantine, abstract, etc.) to express the fear of or hostility towards the natural, and this, in literature, requires a spatial form. Frank does not deny that literature is fundamentally a temporal art, but he claims that at moments it must struggle against its own nature.

> Just as the dimension of depth has vanished from the sphere of visual creation, so the dimension of historical depth has vanished from the content of major works of modern literature. Past and present are apprehended spatially, locked in a timeless unity that, while it may accentuate surface differences, eliminates any feeling of sequence by the very act of juxtaposition. (59)

Frank does not extend his analyses to all literature, or even to all modern literature. He regards the literature in which spatial form is evident as a "limit-case," "an intensification and accentuation of potentialities present in literature almost from the start" (1977:251), which must be united with the literature of temporal form in a more general theory. Several attempts at a

---

[3] For discussions of Worringer's theory, see Wellek and Warren: 211, and especially Hulme: 82–90, as well as Frank, 1963.

unified theory of form have been made,[4] which have tended to expand the significance of Frank's theory to all literature, and to a general theory of representation (semiology). Thus all narrative, as literature and as one kind of representation, is seen as both spatially and temporally formed, and both spatial and temporal form must take part in the understanding of narrative. However, depending upon various cultural factors—and perhaps others: e.g., genre, personal inclination, etc.—one or the other formal factor will predominate. In the literature of spatial form, Frank claims,

> the synchronic [spatial] relations *within* the text took precedence over diachronic referentiality, and . . . it was only after the pattern of synchronic relations had been grasped as a unity that the "meaning" of the poem could be understood. Naturally, to work out such synchronic relations involves the time-act of reading; but the temporality of this act is no longer coordinated with the dominant structural elements of the text. Temporality becomes, as it were, a purely physical limit of apprehension, which conditions but does not determine the work and whose expectations are thwarted and superseded by the space-logic of synchronicity. (1977:235, emphasis Frank's)

W. J. T. Mitchell claims that reading transforms the spatiality of the narrative form into temporality (1980:550). This suggests the possibility that the spatiality belongs to what we have called the narrated, and that it conflicts with the temporality of narration—e.g., our tendency to read the printed words in a linear sequence. This is similar to Eric Rabkin's suggestion that spatial form "defamiliarizes"* the original temporality of story within the reading experience (254–55, 270). If this is so, spatial form appears as a distortion of or deviation from a fundamental temporality of experience, caused perhaps by the sort of cultural factors which Worringer indicated. We remain within the general outlines of a theory of temporal form as developed by Aristotle and Lessing, and we affirm the priority of narration over narrated.

This returns us to the paradoxes of Zeno. What if we reject the assumption of a primary temporality, so predominant in modern thought? Plato presents us, in the *Timaeus*, with an image of a

---

[4] See, for example, the articles by Rabkin, Holtz, and Mitchell.

primordial space, within which time, as "an everlasting likeness
[of eternity] moving according to number" (37d), emerges by the
formative activity of the Demiurge. As we have noted previously,
temporal form has its own, restricted spatiality of the linear sequence. Instead of viewing spatial form as that which disrupts and
distorts this linearity—that which "explodes" it—could we not
view linearity as that which controls and confines the ("eternal")
multiplicity of space—that which "conforms" the originally fragmentary? (cf. Mitchell, 1980:542–43). This, to be sure, reverses all
the assumptions which we so readily and easily make, and it
restores that which is incontrovertibly spatial in narrative, the
signifying material—the written page, the reverberating sound:
the difference which makes language possible[5]—to our theoretical
attention. Thus spatial form, as Frank says, makes us aware of the
fundamental spatiality of narrative, but this means that temporal
form obscures that spatiality.

We can now return to the limits of story which were suggested in Chapter One. On the one hand, there is the beholder,
that which is beyond the metaphysics of story and which intends
the story as a meaningful identity of content and context. It is that
which dwells in the true time of Heidegger and/or the duration of
Bergson, and which can never be present, but only represented, in
story. Thus Heidegger says that "language is the house of
Being"—Bachelard discusses in detail the metaphysics of the spatial image of the house—and that "language holds back its own
origin" (1971a:5, 81). On the other hand is the hyletic* matter of
the sign, also beyond the metaphysics of story in the "opposite
direction,"[6] that which pulls the story apart into utter non-identity
and meaninglessness—the labyrinthine self-referentiality of story.
It dwells in a pure space, which must be suppressed and controlled
when the beholder—like the Platonic Demiurge—transforms it
into the spatialized time (or temporalized space) of story. At this
point it enters the realm of metaphysics.

---

[5] See Frank, 1978: 289–90. See also Calloud: 44; Ingarden: 305–7.

[6] As we noted in Chapter One, there is something resembling an "identity"
between the two limits of story: the sign and the beholder.

3. Space in the Garden[7]

In considering the theological and metaphysical aspects and implications of this theory of narrative form, we must give further support to the claims (1) that Heideggerian/Bergsonian time does not, strictly speaking, belong within the metaphysical realm of story, and (2) that spatial form is not a special case or distortion of linear temporal form, but rather forms the (suppressed) basis for it. These two points cannot be proven here, but they can be supported by an example which I choose both for its theological importance and also because it lies (as a central metaphor*) at the heart of Vernon's argument about space and time in literature: Genesis 2:4b–3:24.

Although Frank clearly indicates that spatial form is more appropriate to modern story than is temporal form, he implies that this may have been true of other times and cultures as well. One thinks of so-called "primitive" myths, and Frank speaks of modern literature "transmuting the time-world of history into the timeless world of myth . . . that finds its appropriate aesthetic expression in spatial form" (1963:60; also 1978:278). And what of Rudolf Bultmann's description—following Juelicher—of parable as similitude (spatial juxtaposition) presented in narrative (temporal) form? We will consider further the spatial form of parable in Chapter Five.

In what sense is the story of the Garden of Eden a myth? A myth is a basic story that explains why and how things are the way they are. Every person has such a basic story, even if he or she has never thought about it or "spelled it out." Each of our stories—our myths—interact with the stories of other human beings; all share to a greater or lesser degree in common myths

---

[7] The following discussion of the story of the Garden of Eden should not be regarded as a complete account of that story, but only of the narrative form of it. Because of the very problematic issues of translation, noted in Chapters One and Five, the story under consideration is limited to the Revised Standard Version account; other versions will be considered only to assist our understanding of the RSV. Whether my conclusions apply to other versions (including of course the Hebrew) will have to be determined separately. For arguments similar to mine, see the articles in *Semeia 18* by Jobling, Patte and Parker, and Boomershine; also Andrew Martin, "The Genesis of Ignorance: Nescience and Omniscience in the Garden of Eden," in *Philosophy and Literature*, Spring, 1981 (Volume 5, No. 1): 3–20. The most brilliant exegesis of the passage of which I am aware is Franz Kafka's "Paradise."

which determine basic intellectual and emotional positions, such as the myths of the Judeo-Christian tradition, of which the story of the Garden of Eden is one. To tell a story involves an act of faith; if I believe in a myth, then I take it as true. When people disagree irreconcilably, it may be because they have adopted irreconcilable myths, not because they have adopted conflicting positions within the same myth. This distinction between two types of ethical disagreement is a very important one.[8]

We need myths because reality—however that is understood—does not conform to logic. We cannot understand all of reality through a unified logical system. We noted, in the previous chapter, the incompleteness theorems of Kurt Gödel, which claim that any finite, logical system—any mathematics, science, etc.—will at some point be either incomplete (unable to account for everything) or inconsistent. The totality of one's experience cannot be put together into a total, logical system in which all the parts fit. There are missing pieces, and there are also pieces present (in reality) which don't fit anywhere.

Myth, however, can present a total "picture" of reality, by telling a story. Myth takes the elements of reality—the logical pieces—and assembles them into a narrative built around some central action or conflict. It reconciles the logical oppositions by turning them into the oppositions between characters or locations, which can then be "solved," not logically but through the working out of the plot. It is from the story that the basic truths and values of reality emerge, not, however, because it is more logical than logic, but because it is more deceptive than logic. As we noted in Chapter One, language—and therefore story—is also subject to incompleteness. Myth is the creation of an illusion of completeness (as binary opposition) through the suppression of self-referentiality—i.e., spatial form. We will discuss this in more detail in Chapter Three.

The story of the Garden of Eden is preceded in the book of Genesis by another myth, the story of God creating the world in six days; these two myths conflict with each other. Perhaps the most glaring conflict is that in the first story, God creates plants and animals first, and then man, and in the second story, man is created first, then plants, then animals. The Garden of Eden

8 Cf. Charles Stevenson's distinction between agreement in belief and agreement in attitude.

story does not begin, as it were, on the eighth day of creation; the stories give two different pictures of the world. Whether this conflict of temporal orders is fundamental or simply a difference of perspective on the same "thing" will not be considered here. Another conflict is that in the first story, God creates everything by speaking—"Let there be light," etc.—and in the Garden of Eden story, God molds the dust—with hands?—and breathes on it. God appears to have a body. In the first story, God is temporal; he creates time, and he creates in time. In the second story, God creates space, and in space. The story of the Garden of Eden is a spatial story, a story in which spatial form predominates. Although there is movement and action—temporality—in the Garden of Eden story, time does not pass; the action is defined spatially, not temporally. We are in a world outside of time, or before time. Time only begins when this story ends.

The story begins by establishing a point in space, the point of creation. "The Lord God formed man of dust from the ground, and breathed into his nostrils the breath of life" (2:7). God molds the man out of dust, out of the lifeless muck, much as a potter works clay. One readily envisions this God as a material, spatial being; later on, we are told that God walks in the Garden. Can we speak of a God who creates space without also spatializing God, giving him a body?

God gives life by breathing on the man of dust. The life of a human is his or her "breath" or "spirit," which according to the story comes from God. Human creators also breathe their spirit into the things they form, the works of their hands. This breathing or inspiration is a spatial inhabiting of the material soil, and creativity and life itself are established in the story as fundamentally spatial. God, at this point, resembles the Platonic Demiurge, but there are striking differences as well.

The Garden is placed in the east: where the sun rises, where time begins? Perhaps it simply means beyond all knowledge. It is important, however, that it is given a place, a location. The Garden fills a space, even if the location of that space is presently unknown, or if the space is "only" symbolic. The man is put in the Garden. The Garden encloses the man; it surrounds him. It establishes a place of security, a place of life. We do not have to go as far as Freud did and think of such a space as a cosmic womb. The French philosopher Gaston Bachelard has demonstrated the metaphysical importance of any structure which establishes an inside and an outside, such as a shell, a nest, or especially a house. The inside is always intimate; it is safe and warm (1964:100–101). The outside is threatening and dangerous. The inside is rational, organized, a meaningful world; the outside is irrational and chaotic. What is created in the Eden story is not a forest, nor a wilderness, but a Garden. There are many different types of garden, but they are all cultivated places. They are all artificial, fabricated; they are arranged according to a plan. A garden is always the result of techniques, of technology. Scholars have noted that the man's labors—and of course God's—inside the Garden are given a positive value in the story, in contrast to the man's (later) labors outside of the Garden. The Garden is an enclosed orchard, a Paradise. As the story tells us later on, outside of the Garden lie (accursed) labor, pain, and death.

The Garden is the meaningful, human world. From the Garden proceed the four great rivers that water the world—the world that the ancient Hebrew people knew. The rivers carry life from the Garden out into the world, and therefore the Garden stands symbolically at the center of the universe. This may remind us of other ancient myths which hold that a great pillar or mountain stands in the middle of the earth. In Norse mythology, it is the great cosmic tree, Yggdrasill, with its roots in the underworld and its branches supporting the heavens.

In the Garden, however, there are two trees, which are not as great as Yggdrasill perhaps, but of immense importance. According to the story, they are in the midst of the Garden: "the tree of life also in the midst of the garden, and the tree of the knowledge of good and evil" (2:9b).[9] This means that the Garden has two centers: its unity is disrupted. Biblical scholarship is troubled by this duality and explains it historically as the result of the incomplete combination of two stories into the canonical version. These are an ancient, polytheistic (spatial) Eden-myth and a later, monotheistic (temporal) creation account (Von Rad; Westermann; Köhler). The present approach neither confirms

---

[9] Both the Jerusalem Bible and New English Bible use "middle." Jobling argues that the tree of knowledge, belonging semantically to the outside of the Garden, is in tension with the tree of life. This would establish what I call in Chapter Five an oscillation between outside and inside.

nor disputes this; however, instead of explaining away the duality as an historical awkwardness, it takes it as an essential element of the canonical story.[10] To be sure, the Garden is watered by the one river (which again comes from "the east")[11] and it is created by the one God, and it encloses the one man. But already in the moment of creation, there is introduced a duality, a polarity. The Garden, the source and center of reality, is divided by its two centers.

What is this split? The trees are of the knowledge of good and evil, and of life, respectively. Thus we have symbolically a split between knowledge—moral knowledge, but to the Hebrew mind, all practical knowledge—and life, or to put it into more philosophical terms, between existence and essence. It is the gap or difference between the ability—and necessity—to decide, on the one hand, and the possession of one's self, on the other, as we learn later in the story. It is the separation between moral freedom and immortality. It is because of this separation between knowledge and life that the eating of the forbidden fruit can so disrupt and disorder human life (cf. Jobling: 47).

The story of the Garden of Eden is therefore constructed upon two spatial structures: a structure of enclosure (the body within the Garden), and a structure of division (the separated trees). The form of the narrative is determined by the tension between these structures as one of discomfort, of "not fitting." This represents the human condition as one of alienation or estrangement from the world, expressed in the gap between the

[10] The present approach draws heavily not only on Bachelard and Frank, but also on the structuralist theory of myth of C. Lévi-Strauss (as developed by J. D. Crossan [1975, 1976, 1980]). Vernon's analysis of the story has also been helpful.

[11] Cf. Boomershine: 116. Is there a relation between this one, unnamed river and its four offshoots, and the Greek *Oceanos*, the river flowing endlessly around the world, without beginning or end? Is Ouroboros, the serpent which inhabits Oceanos (or is identical with it)—the snake devouring its own tail—somehow related to the serpent in the Garden? I.e., does the serpent belong to the one river-source of the Garden? Does the serpent then represent God, or rather, a fundamental division within God, corresponding to the divided trees, etc.? Cf. Crossan in *Semeia* 18: 109. (Crossan also implies the spatial importance of the two trees [110].) Later in the story, God apparently lies to the man about the consequences of eating the fruit, but the serpent tells Eve the truth. Also, how could the human image (breath) of God be divided, if the original were not already split? Cf. Patte and Parker: 71; Vernon: 3.

ability to choose and the destiny which emerges from the choices made.[12]

Christian theologians have described this alienation as "original sin," the crime committed by Adam and Eve later in this story. They have ignored the fact that the separation occurs much earlier in the story; it occurs in the creation by God of the Garden itself. It is God who creates the Garden and puts the trees in it; it is from God that alienation—the separation between knowledge and life—comes. This separation is built into the very fabric of the universe, because the Garden at its center itself has two centers and cannot be a unity.

If there had only been one tree—if knowledge and life were united—then when the humans ate its fruit, they would have become gods.[13] The revolution of mankind against God which is narrated in this story would have succeeded. As it is, with the two trees, the revolution must fail. This duality built into the universe condemns the human attempt to become God to failure.

> We are sinful not merely because we have eaten of the Tree of Knowledge, but also because we have not yet eaten of the Tree of Life. The state in which we find ourselves is sinful, quite independent of guilt. (Kafka: 29)

The central portion of the story consists of the plot, that which for Aristotelian theory—for any theory of a primary temporal form—as well as for traditional Christian theology, forms the core, the central action of the story. Here linear time—past, present, future—seems to occur. However, based upon the preceding, this action appears to be nothing more than the inevitable unfolding of the spatial structures of the Garden itself. To put it into somewhat different language, in traditional literary theory, a story is generated from the inside—the central event—outwards. I am arguing that this story is generated from the outside—the spatial forms at the beginning (and again at the end)—inwards. This metaphorical* distinction is crucial to the question of the metaphysics of story. To the extent that the story

---

12 Cf. Albert Camus, The Fall.

13 It is argued that in the earlier form of the Eden-myth, Adam and Eve were gods, and so were the trees (or the one tree, of life) (Köhler, von Rad). "Before the gods existed, the woods were sacred, and the gods came to dwell in these sacred woods. All they did was to add human, all too human, characteristics to the great law of forest revery" (Bachelard, 1964:186).

is a metaphysical entity, an identity, it must establish itself around a unitary center.[14] To the extent that it escapes into the multiplicity of a pure spatiality, it does not resolve its identity and thus—strictly speaking—it is not "a story" (despite what is written above), but rather many possible stories. We must note that this opposition (in the narration) between one metaphysical entity (the centered plot) and a dispersed spatiality corresponds exactly to the (narrated) opposition between the one Garden and the two trees. The story is itself an enclosure, disrupted by a dual center. This is the self-referentiality of the story, its representation of and hence separation from itself—its non-identity. This structure dislocates the sense of the story (as we noted regarding Frege's theory of meaning in Chapter One) and therefore short-circuits its referentiality, making possible, as we shall see, the polysemy of the story.

Within this central "action," spatiality continues to operate. The man is given the power to name the animals, and the significance of naming as creative power in an oral culture has long been noted; we find it echoed in Socrates's concern for the spoken word, noted in the previous chapter.[15] Naming is, however, the power to differentiate and separate; its function is far more spatial than temporal.

Because the man is "alone," God divides him into two beings, and it is only after this point that the names Adam and Eve appear;[16] up to this point, the first human is simply called "the man." We cannot deal here with the chauvinism of the English and Hebrew languages, nor do any more than note that the story itself appears to suggest that "the man" (prior to separation of male and female) is androgynous.[17] We are in any case

---

[14] See Bachelard, 1964, *passim*.

[15] See Walter Ong, *The Presence of the Word*.

[16] And then only at the moment of the curses. The Jerusalem and New English Bible are even more cautious about using the name "Adam," although the Septuagint uses it very freely. "Adam" is a transformation of the Hebrew *'dm*, which is being punned with *'dmh* (the ground from which he is formed). "The man" is never given a proper name in the Hebrew account. The translation of a story into another language, while ideally the same as the original, inevitably differs from it; translation is always an act of violence. See note 9.

[17] If the first man is androgynous, what of the "second Adam"? "In Christ . . . there is neither male nor female" (Gal. 3:26–28). Like Paradise, the state of salvation consists of an undisturbed spatial unity. Cf. Bachelard, 1969:85, 188, and Plato, *The Symposium*: 336.

not concerned here with the realm of beings studied by empirical biology. I only wish to point out that we have here another spatial split, another division in the Garden. Why would God create a lonely man? Why couldn't God have made the man so that he/she was self-sufficient? Is it possible that this separation of the sexes reflects the earlier separation of knowledge and life? Once the principle of duality has been introduced into the universe (and at its source), must it not inexorably fracture every thing in it? Must not every thing be separated from itself, just as the man is now separated from him/herself? Has this separation spread throughout reality?

From the separation between male and female, the ultimate separation follows inevitably. It is not, however, a "new" separation, but rather it reflects and continues the others. First there is the spatial and ontological separation of the two trees, then the human and sexual separation of Adam and Eve, and finally, the ethical and psychological separation of the crime—the eating of the forbidden fruit—and the resulting guilt and shame. Each one unfolds into the next one. Can we imagine this last separation without the previous ones? The sinful revolt of the human beings arises from the frustration of a desire for unity, from the split which establishes their dual existence. Thus revolt, duality, and the acquisition of knowledge are opposed to harmony, unity, and innocence.[18]

The result of the crime is that the humans put on rudimentary clothes and hide. Original nakedness is innocence; it is non-separation, full self-presence, as opposed to the difference of alienation. The symbol for human alienation from one another is clothes, in which we continually hide ourselves from ourselves and from one another. Our clothes are artificial enclosures, substitute Gardens, with which we surround ourselves, to protect ourselves; they create, as the Garden did, an inside and an outside, an ordered world. Clothes are metaphysical.[19] They manipulate reality; they establish a universe. We might say that the human pair reject God's Garden and create a garden of their own. This rejection of God, turning away from God to establish a world of one's own, is what traditional Christian theology has

---

[18] "Hell is other people" (Sartre, *No Exit*).
[19] Cf. White: 104. Also see the work of Roland Barthes on the semiology of garments.

meant by "original sin," the sin which infects all human beings. Sin, in imitation of the original creative act, is also spatial. Do we have here the beginnings of a biblical theory of representation? Yet the theological focus upon its originality overlooks the mimesis and heightens the temporality of the story.

God walks in the Garden and does not know where or why the humans are hiding. The "action" has ended and spatiality again comes to the fore. There is a gap between the pair and God, which limits both the humans and God, and which becomes, when they hide themselves, ignorance and estrangement. Story is a sequence of spatial arrangements, and in this case, the spatial arrangements continually threaten to escape from the sequential control. It is exactly the opposite in the creation story in Genesis 1, where for theological and perhaps other reasons, temporal sequence uniformly orders the spatial elements.

The story of the Garden of Eden began with a blessing, the act of creation. However, unlike the first creation story, which both begins and ends with a blessing—"behold, it was very good"—this story ends with curses. The man, whose creation was a blessing and for whom the Garden was a blessing, is now Adam and Eve, who are cursed. There is a tragic reversal of position, a spatial reversal. The man was in the midst of the Garden; Adam and Eve will be thrust from the Garden. They move from inside the enclosure, from life and satisfaction, to the outside, to pain, frustration, and death. The separation already present in the creation of the two trees now runs through all of reality, and with the curses, the metaphysical enclosure of the Garden is burst open.

It is, however, replaced by a new space. The curses are spatial: the serpent crawling upon the ground, the female bringing forth children, the male toiling upon the ground and eventually returning to it (when the breath abandons the dust which had enclosed it). The three serve as scapegoats, sacrificial victims establishing the fundamental difference between human and divine, in contrast to the original crisis or confusion of man and God (the singleness of "breath," the eating of forbidden fruit). Adam and Eve have become (too much?) "like God." The original spatial relation of harmony and peace is replaced by a new spatiality of struggling and discord. The garden which the humans sought to create for themselves is now thrust upon them with a vengeance, symbolized by the new clothes which God himself makes for them.

In the Garden, the humans may not have been necessarily immortal, like God, but they were at least contingently immortal: death was not inevitable. The banishment and curse make death inevitable, because access to the tree of life is now cut off (cf. Kafka: 31). Death is no longer an option but now a requirement, and this makes it bitter. Similarly, labor, which was good in the Garden, is bitter on the outside of it.

Thus the Garden gives violent birth to the human species. If the Garden were everything, then when the humans were banished, it would have been destroyed (cf. Kafka: 29). If, however, it is the center of reality, the spatially metaphysical ordering principle, then the humans need only to be thrust outside, beyond its security and warmth, into the chaos beyond.

A guardian with a flaming sword is placed between the humans and the Garden. The guardian is also "in the east"—a symbolic direction, since we are told that the sword's protection "turned every way." Again, the east may represent that which is lost forever; there is no going back to the Garden.

However, to speak about going back, or not going back, is now to speak about history. The Garden is located in a symbolic space, not to be found in any non-symbolic search—a space "at the beginning" of linear time. History begins when humanity leaves the space of the Garden. How could history exist where death was not necessary? The sun might rise and set; we might even imagine the second hand sweeping around the face of a clock. "Spatialized time" might very well exist in the Garden. If so, it would only be because of the spatiality of the heavens or of the clock mechanism, just as the movements of the human pair in the Garden are possible only because of the space of the two trees. However, the time of Heidegger and Bergson would not exist there. If death were not inevitable, how would one moment be any different than the next? Endless time would collapse every one of its moments into nothing; there could be no exstases, no duration.

However, each human being expects this life to end sooner or later. Each moment passed is a moment lost; it can never be retrieved or made up for. Each moment carries us one step—one linear unit—closer to the last moment, and it is therefore immensely important. We cannot go back; as Bergson says, duration is irreversible (1949:62). However, so is linear time. The irreversibility of our duration presses us toward a metaphysics of linearity,

of the reality of history as temporal form. History exists for us. It is
the guardian of the Garden, standing between its gates and
humanity. The Garden of Eden lies just one instant before our
story begins: very close, but infinitely far away. The Garden of
Eden exists before history, or better, outside of history, for history
is determined by it as also a sort of (metaphysical) enclosure. History is the pain and frustration and death—the linearity—that is
outside of the Garden. The Garden is artificial, unnatural; outside
of it lies the natural realm of history, linear time. The story juxta-
poses a spatial realm of difference with the linear time of identity;
yet the historical realm is the consequence of sin and falsehood.

4. The Implications of Narrative Form

Thus there is a map at the heart of the garden. Our examination of the story of the Garden of Eden indicates that it is fundamentally spatial, and that Heideggerian/Bergsonian time is
"foreign" to it, in the sense of a continual pressure to suppress
and transform its spatiality into a linear temporality. Does this
mean that all stories, insofar as they are meaningful, metaphysical entities, must be so transformed? If this were so, it would be
impossible to perform the sort of analyses that I have attempted
above, and that Frank, Vernon, and others have done with
works of modern literature. The fact that we can become conscious of this spatiality suggests a sort of "resistance" of the sign
to this pressure from the beholder. Some stories may give more
resistance than others, and some readers or hearers may be more
sensitive to this resistance than others. Therefore the notion of
spatial form remains controversial.

The "pure spatialization" of a story is no doubt inapprehendable—except as a theoretical limit—in the same way that the
hyletic phase of the sign is inapprehendable as such. If it were
apprehendable, it would destroy the story as such; therefore, the
more labyrinthine stories become—e.g., the parables of Borges or
Kafka—the less recognizable they are as stories. For similar
reasons, the "pure temporalization" of stories is also inapprehendable, and if it were apprehended, would destroy the story.
The story would be destroyed and become immediate, non-
reflective (non-conceptual) consciousness, if that is possible. These
are the two extremes which Bergson noted, the dispersion and the
concentration of duration, between which lies metaphysics.

Therefore stories, as metaphysical entities, may be described as more or less linear, more or less multidimensional. We have already noted the contrast between the two creation stories in Genesis. This returns us to the distinction between the auditory (oral) and the visual (pictorial), except that in this light they are not discontinuous sensory realms, but rather significantly distinct points on a continuum which runs from the infinitesimal to the infinite, and which is determined by both the beholder and the material sign.

The implications of this distinction are important. The theologian Lonnie Kliever has argued that there are "affinites between 'temporal' narratives and *historical* religions" (549, emphasis Kliever's). He concludes that "'spatial' narrative lends itself to the shaping of either *mystic* or *polytheistic* religious sensibilities" (552, emphasis Kliever's). Paul Tillich has argued along very similar lines, relating spatially-oriented religions to tragedy, idolatry, polytheism, and nationalism, and relating temporally-oriented religions (the Judeo-Christian tradition) to human triumph over tragedy and injustice, to the prophetic tradition, and to monotheism.

> Human existence under the predominance of space is tragic. Greek tragedy and philosophy knew about this. They knew that the Olympic gods were gods of space, one beside the other, one struggling with the other. Even Zeus was only the first of many equals, and hence subject, together with man and the other gods, to the tragic law of genesis and decay. (33)

> The God of time is the God of history. This means, first of all, that He is the God who acts in history towards a final goal. History has a direction, something new is to be created in it and through it. . . . The tragic circle of space is overcome. There is a definite beginning and a definite end in history. (37)

Strikingly similar claims concerning nationalism and idolatry have been made against the literary theory of spatial form, to which Frank has responded, it seems to me, quite effectively (1977:247–50; 1978:276–77). Tillich is quite clearly thinking of the divisibility of space—each god with his/her own geographical locale—as opposed to the non-divisibility (unless we suppose a sequence of unitary gods) of time. As we noted in the analysis of the Garden of Eden story, God almost necessarily acquires a body, and he can be separated from his creations, who then can hide from him, in that story. Spatial form demands incarnation. In contrast, in Genesis 1, God is pure disembodied "voice," and thereby lord of and present to all of the creation.

However, there is another, related way in which this theological distinction is appropriate. If the story has a linear, temporal form, then it has a metaphysical identity, which is its meaning. As it is one story, it can only have one meaning, which is either understood correctly or not. This notion of a single, true meaning as the correct understanding of any story has dominated both secular and theological hermeneutics since the end of the medieval period, and it appears to be both theoretically and historically linked to the notion of a linear temporal form—e.g., Luther's notion of the "plain meaning" of scripture and the historical-critical search for the "author's intent" as the key to the meaning of a text. In contrast, the theory of spatial form has been theoretically linked with the structuralists' assertion of the polysemy of stories: the great variety of meanings that can emerge from variations within a synchronic structure (Holtz: 276; Frank, 1978). The spatiality of the Garden of Eden story is its tendency to split (as the Garden itself does) and become many different stories, and this—far from being idolatrous—suggests a radical iconoclasm, as has been well-argued by John Dominic Crossan (1976, 1980). There is no one, true meaning when the story begins to dissolve in its spatiality, and therefore it eludes metaphysical identity.

The structuralists distinguish between diachronic (linear temporal) and synchronic structures, which in the story become the syntagm, or sequence of signs, and the paradigm, or possible transformations of a given sign within the "same" story. The identity of the story is determined by the syntagm, and the paradigm, by differing sufficiently from a canonical syntagm, diffuses its identity; yet the paradigm contains the possibility of its meanings. Might we then speak of Christianity, Judaism, and Islam, as "historical" religions, as being primarily syntagmatic—that is, as having suppressed the paradigmatic elements of difference? In their search for doctrinal, canonical identity, they have tended to ignore the spatial, paradigmatic, polytheistic possibilities of story and to focus entirely on a temporal form—in, for example, their own foundational myths, such as the story of the Garden of Eden. These religions thus stand in an almost self-contradictory position.

Within the tradition of the historical religions, it is the discipline of theology (as well, as Kliever notes, as the practice of the mystics) which has maintained the paradigmatic elements. This is no doubt in part due to theology's Platonic origins as the search for the eternally true amid the flux of existence. However, it is also a result of the tension between the syntagmatic and the paradigmatic—the self-contradiction noted above—that theology almost inevitably engages with heresy. It is essentially "polytheistic."

Aristotle claimed that poetry is closer to philosophy (universal ideas) than it is to history (specific facts) (1451b); to determine a beginning, a middle, and an end is to choose some matters and to reject others. Any story can only tell some things, and never everything; otherwise it ceases to be a story. What is not told is, in a sense, just as crucial to the story as what is told. All narratives are temporally incomplete (Chatman: 29).

Within this framework, "belief" appears as an act of selection. The Garden of Eden stands forever closed to us, guarded by an angelic being with a flaming sword. Nonetheless, the story of the Garden can inform our stories; it can direct them by the ways in which we draw upon it. If I believe myself to be a child of Eve, to use C. S. Lewis's elegant phrase, then Eve's story is a part of my story. Although the (narrated) Garden remains untouched by history, its story can reach into history, as narration. It can become incarnate in my story.[20]

Hermeneutics, then, is not something to be applied upon or added to the story; understanding begins with the choice of story itself. Story is selection—a given story intends a world, or we intend the world in the story—and therefore it is meaningful. The Greeks saw the poets as fabricators or creators of worlds—Demiurges; more recently, Crossan has claimed that it is only in terms of story that we may speak of a world (1975). The act of determining that "this is a story"—the twin questions of canon and value—is the act of discovering or receiving or creating a meaningful world. The story is the meaning itself, and it is impossible to know or hear or tell a story apart from its meaning.

This meaning frames a content with a context. It constitutes the story as "this story," and it is to this source that the story's form must be traced. Our understanding of space and time, the

---

[20] See my *Theology as Comedy*, Chapter Seven. Cf. Mitchell, 1980:562.

forms of our existence, proceeds from this selection; every hermeneutics is also at least implicitly a cosmology. Prior to the choice of story—human beings never actually experience this priority—there are only empty words, the hyletic phase of the sign. Upon being chosen, constituted as story, the words point to a world, which is our world, for we have chosen it. In constituting the story as a world, we also constitute the beholder as ourselves, as the "other side" of the same act (cf. Phillips: 135). In choosing a story, we choose meaning. All understanding and interpretation must be referred to this act of choice.

We are not likely, of course, consciously to choose a meaning, nor do we choose temporality or spatiality. As Rudolf Arnheim has argued, time and space do not normally appear to our immediate awareness, but only through an act of reflective abstraction. What we choose is a story.[21] Yet there is no simple identity between story and meaning. We all do not find the same meaning in the "same" story; perhaps it might then be argued that it is not really the same story. The story is more than any one meaning; it carries the potential to negate, by means of one of its meanings, any other meanings that may be chosen. As we noted earlier, the language resists and frustrates our attempts to establish an interpretation; it is inexhaustibly opaque.

Time and space come into existence in story as ranges of potential meaning within it, expressions of the power of story. They express the meaningful tension between content and context, the fact that it is in story that reality becomes a world and a self. Seen in terms of the indefinitely plural significance of story, theology participates in the creation of the world and the self and expresses man's collaboration with God in existence itself. For theology as story, the world is still uncreated; nature and history are potentialities hidden within a silent reality, awaiting a storyteller to call them forth and an audience to incarnate them.

Theology as story cannot look upon the universe of time and space as fixed frameworks within which it is confined. The data

[21] We never actually exist without a story—i.e. without a world. Our being-in-the-world is always existentially and conceptually prior to the pre-hermeneutics or non-world which by being chosen becomes story/world, and which can only be encountered as the resistance to meaning of the sign. Cf. Sartre, n.d.:269–70, 1956:14–16.

of "everyday reality" are not simply what they seem. Nor are we allowed to pretend that they are anything we want. We must proceed, then, to an examination of the metaphysics of fiction and reality, the referentiality of story, and the nature of belief.

Chapter Three
BELIEFS, FICTIONS, AND FACTS

1. Christological Fantasy: An Example

We ordinarily recognize that there are some intellectual forms that we commonly call "fictions," and there are some intellectual forms that we commonly call, by way of distinction, "facts" or "truths" or "realities." We also recognize that the line between fact and fiction is not at all clear and that there are many ambiguous cases. It may be that by exploring these ambiguities we can clarify the connection, or lack of same, between fact and fiction, and the metaphysics of that distinction.

The theological fictions of Swedish novelist and playwright Pär Lagerkvist provide an approach to exploring the ambiguity between fact and fiction. They include excellent examples of what Jorge Luis Borges has called "christological fantasies." A christological fantasy is a systematic statement about the Christ which is presented in a fictional context. Christological fantasy should be clearly distinguished from the use of "Christ-figures" or Christian images or even of christological themes in literature or in the arts. All of these may have christological implications, but they are not usually as explicit or as systematic as christological fantasy, nor do they raise the question of fact and fiction so well. Christological fantasy also excludes what Theodore Ziolkowski has called fictional transfigurations of the Christ, which tend to reflect the author's own christology. Christological fantasy is not a genre, although it is perhaps more likely to be found in those anti-Aristotelian literary forms in which thought predominates over plot.*

Borges used the term originally in reference to his own story, "Three Versions of Judas," which is about a (Swedish!) theologian who comes by a gradual and oddly logical series of biblical researches to the conclusion that it was Judas, not Jesus, who was the Messiah. The christology which Borges presents in this story is clearly a fiction. The reader does not take it to be Borges's own belief, nor are we inclined to think because of it that any actual person has ever held this belief (although it does carry, Borges notes, overtones of Gnosticism). Yet there is nothing within the christology itself that marks it as any less real or factual than any other christology; only the context of its being believed by a fictional character does so. Thus we are not inclined to take it as seriously as we would take those christologies which emerge from the stories of actual, existing people, including of course the christologies of real theologians and of the creeds which real people have believed. Perhaps this reflects the Judeo-Christian theological commitment to the reality of history, the linear temporality of which we spoke in the preceding chapter. But history, too, is "only" a story, as are all of our individual stories. If we follow this line of argumentation, we are guilty of a kind of circularity, in which stories are categorized as factual or fictional in terms of a meta-story,* which itself must then be categorized, etc. We normally (and unconsciously) break this circle by accepting the meta-story—whether it be the Judeo-Christian tradition or some alternate account—uncritically.

In two of Lagerkvist's best-known works in English, *Barabbas* and *The Sibyl*, we are presented with three christological fantasies. (Actually, in *Barabbas* several christologies are offered, but only one, that of the title character, predominates and incorporates the others.) Two of the christologies center upon Jesus of Nazareth, and the third centers upon an incarnate son of the Greek god Dionysus. Despite the important differences between these christologies, the reader is perhaps more likely to take them seriously, and even as Lagerkvist's own beliefs, than in the case of Borges's story. Yet given their context, they are just as fictional as the christology of Borges's story.

Barabbas is the one person who could say with certainty that Christ had died for him. In this sense, he can be far more factual than the modern Christian, whose claim in that respect is highly metaphorical* by comparison. Barabbas is an eye-witness to both the crucifixion and the resurrection, but more important, Jesus, for him, is the one who postponed his own death and thereby added more years of misery to his life. This one empirical datum forms the core of his christology and is given to the reader at the beginning of the novel; the remainder of Barabbas's christology is far more nebulous and emerges slowly and painfully throughout the rest of his life-story. Barabbas's story is of a suspended death-sentence which is eventually fulfilled, of a man terrified and yet fascinated by the darkness and nothingness of death. He is perplexed by a son of god who cannot prevent his own, particularly disgusting, death—who is weakness incarnate—and he is annoyed by the ineffectual love of the Christians. Faith continually escapes Barabbas, and each time that he or others reach for it, it brings about destruction and confusion; it is the stuff of ignorance. And yet at his death, he speaks "into the darkness, as though he were speaking to it" the dying words of Christ, "To thee I deliver up my soul" (1951:180). Barabbas is a Christ-figure, but a Christ modeled upon his own christology: a Christ whose actions, both good and evil, occur in spite of himself, a failed Christ, a Christ whose only salvation, if we can call it that, lies in reconciliation with the ultimate darkness, in joining the "brotherhood of the crucified."[1]

In *The Sibyl*, Jesus is presented in a different manner. A nameless wanderer, later identified as Ahasuerus, tells a story of being damned by Christ to everlasting life when he refused to allow Jesus, carrying his cross to Calvary, to rest his head momentarily on the side of his house. His punishment is to wander forever, seeking rest and finding none. Christ is unforgiving and even spiteful: how was Ahasuerus to know that he was not some common criminal?

The man tells his story to an old woman, a former pythia or sibyl of the oracle at Delphi, and she answers him with a story of her own. In her ritual intoxication, she had been violated by the goat-god and had borne a son, severely retarded, who is now a grown man and who hunches in the corner of her hut, smiling idiotically. The woman has tried throughout her life to persuade herself that he is the child of her human lover, a man who died at the moment that she was raped by the god, but she comes increasingly to the conviction that he is the god's son. At this point in the novel, the idiot leaves the hut, casts off his human disguise, and ascends from the mountainside into the night sky.

Barabbas understands Christ as an impotent son of god, a loving healer of men's bodies and spirits whose "healing" seems to produce more pain, or at least uncertainty, than was there before. He is an apocalyptic figure who produces expectations which are not only unfulfilled, but which lead to added suffering

[1] Cf. Swanson; Weathers, chapter 5.

and misfortune. Ahasuerus sees Jesus as a magician, a sorceror of no greater moral stature than the average person, using his divine powers for vindictive purposes. The other divine son is beyond all human morality, for he smiles idiotically on good and evil alike. The one is put to death violently at the hands of men, allegedly because of his supernatural mission, and he retaliates by condemning a not-quite-innocent bystander to eternal life (both contrasting to and paralleling Barabbas's last-minute reprieve). The other dwells in isolation from humanity all his life, and he ascends by his own action to his divine father when his human mother almost accidentally reveals his identity to the stranger.

Despite these superficial differences, there are important similarities between these christologies. First, although they are apparently divine, these saviors are all failures. A man whom Jesus had resuscitated tells Barabbas that death is "nothing," and that "to those who have been [dead], nothing else is anything either" (63). Faith is for Barabbas a continual cause of agony and confusion. Jesus grants immortality in *The Sibyl*, but it is by way of damnation, not salvation; again, his effect is to produce unrest and despair. The sibyl's son has no effect on mankind in general; his smile cannot be construed to imply approval of human life (or of anything). Rather, it suggests nothing human at all. His effect on his mother, the one human that he does have contact with, is to remind her constantly of her suffering and grief at the hands of the god.

Second, the three christologies all contain a complex mixture of good and evil. In each case, the Christ is not innocent. This is only suggested in *Barabbas*, where the evils that occur are seen to be the results of Jesus's impotence, and of the expectations that he had aroused. In *The Sibyl*, Jesus is clearly malicious, and the sibyl's son is indifferent—or if at all interested, he is so in a very nonhuman sort of way. In all three cases, misfortune, suffering, and death are not alleviated or surmounted by faith but are caused by it. The god(s) who are "with us" in these incarnations must either be seen as morally incomprehensible or even as positively evil.[2] The sibyl says,

---

[2] The idiotic smile on the face of the sibyl's son reappears again and again in Lagerkvist's stories. It is frequently taken to represent the enigmatic, complex, or indifferent character of God. Cf. Spector (96); Swanson (313); Weathers (19).

> God is merciless. Those who say he is good do not know
> him. He is the most inhuman thing there is. . . . The
> divine is not human; it is something quite different. And
> it is not noble or sublime or spiritualized, as one likes to
> believe. It is alien and repellent and sometimes it is
> madness. It is malignant and dangerous and fatal. (1958:
> 136–37)

Third, these Christs are eternal, or timeless, beings. All three
have appeared in history (the fictionalized "history" of the
novel); yet none of them is confined to history. This is most
clearly seen in the sibyl's son, who though born of a woman—in
a parallel to the Christmas story—can easily cast off his human
form and rise up to heaven. The stories also make it evident,
however, that Jesus, by stealing a man's death from him—as he
does to both Barabbas and Ahasuerus—can separate man from
history, even while he continues to live in it. Jesus reverses the
curse of Adam and Eve, but he does so with another curse. In all
three cases, the correlate of the christology is that history ceases
to matter. It is worth noting here that in the remainder of the
pentalogy of which these novels are the first two,[3] the characters, events, and settings become increasingly abstract and symbolic; the lack of detail and significant intrusions of "authorial
ignorance" (or what Lucien Maury has called "elliptic suggestion" [Lagerkvist, 1951:viii]) which are evident in *Barabbas* and
The Sibyl spiral into pure form, ritualized movement, and
dream-like atmosphere, all of which give to Lagerkvist's stories a
time-less quality. Spatial form predominates in these stories.

These last two christological similarities—lack of innocence
and abstraction from history—are also important in the christological fantasy by Borges noted above. Other contemporary
christological fantasies may also contain one or more of these
characteristics in various combinations. However, I do not want
to suggest that these are somehow essential ingredients to all

---

Lagerkvist, in his essay on "Modern Theatre," makes no explicitly theological
claims, but he does speak of the need to express anguish (Buckman: 19).
Swanson comments that Lagerkvist uses myth to interpret myth (316).

[3] In chronological order: *Barabbas, The Sibyl, The Death of Ahasuerus, Pil-
grim at Sea, The Holy Land.* The later novels contain additional christological
fantasies, culminating in what is sometimes understood to be a reconciliation
(via "empty symbols") of man and God in the brotherhood of the crucified (see
note 1). Yet Spector describes the pentalogy as an endless dialogue of the soul
(119).

christological fantasy; in fact, I suspect that they are not. It may be that these elements can be reduced to some other ones, or that additional elements are possible, and that no one element is necessary. For example, do cultural and historical factors make a difference? They do in the christologies of real people, so perhaps they would also in fictional ones. What effect would generic differences have?

These three points of similarity do, however, raise a further matter. It was claims of this sort that characterized the Gnostic and other heresies; all three of Lagerkvist's christologies could be interpreted as docetic. Perhaps what keeps us from doing that is our awareness that they are fictions. For them to be heresies, they would have to be asserted as true, and then they could be refuted as "errors" or "lies"; as long as they are clearly labeled "fiction," we know that they are lies of a more or less acceptable sort and we do not need to refute them. What can transform fiction into lie (or truth), and vice versa? Does the difference between fact and fiction reduce to a matter of social definition and public labeling?

2. Fact and Fiction

Such a distinction, although common, is unacceptable. Different cultures do indeed hold different stories about the world to be true, but they do not disagree so radically that intercultural communication is impossible. At the level of the individual, we are not free to choose whatever account of reality we want; the girl in the movie *Atlantic City* who chooses not to believe in gravity strikes us as ludicrous and silly, but we realize that beliefs like that are very close to insanity. (Fortunately for the girl, she still acts as though she believes in gravity.) The possibility of communication indicates an agreement which limits all relativity, and which lies in the referentiality of language.

To the extent that the distinction between fact and fiction is not clear—or is relative—we must show what the connections between the two are. That they are not two entirely separate realms is indicated by phenomena such as christological fantasy, which can appear within the frame of fiction and yet contain statements believed, or believable, by actual persons. Historical persons, such as Barabbas and Jesus, and historical cultural institutions, such as the Delphic oracle, can also appear in fictions, alongside of "purely" fictitious persons and institutions. These are all, perhaps, somewhat exceptional. Nonetheless, they raise the problem of the connections between fictional and factual entities and relations, and of the metaphysics of these connections: a problem which applies not only to these "exceptional" cases, but to everything fictional.

Both Plato and Aristotle view fiction as an imitation of the actual. For Plato, this is in general a fault, because the actual is itself, he claims, a copy of the eternal forms, and thus fiction, as a copy of a copy, is bound to introduce errors. In *The Republic*, however, Socrates does grant a limited value to stories about the gods and heroic humans, if they can reproduce ideal—chiefly moral—qualities for the indoctrination of society. For Aristotle, *mimesis* means that poetry tends more toward philosophy than history. If we take history as the representation of "what actually happened," then this also means that story, like philosophy, abstracts ideal truths from ordinary experience. Although Aristotle is more positive in his evaluation of poetic fiction than Plato, both agree that the fictional tends (or ought to tend) away from the real (factual) and towards the ideal (universal, eternal). However, as imitation of the actual, fiction does this by drawing upon (in its composition and apprehension) factual elements. Fiction is (or should be) a sort of compromise between the real and the ideal.

Working from a rather different set of presuppositions, David Hume claims that fiction does not consist in an "idea," but in the lack of a "sentiment or feeling" which is attached to all beliefs that something is a fact,

> and which depends not on the will, nor can be commanded at pleasure. It must be excited by nature, like all other sentiments; and must arise from the particular situation, in which the mind is placed at any particular juncture. (31)

> All belief of matter of fact or real existence is derived merely from some object, present to the memory or senses, and a customary conjunction between that and some other object. (30)

Because of these conjunctions, through the principles of association in the mind, we are able to imagine an absent friend, when we sense (in actuality) something customarily conjoined with him or her.[4] Fiction arises in the imagination, which

> though it cannot exceed that original stock of [sensory] ideas, . . . it has unlimited power of mixing, compounding, separating, and dividing these ideas. . . . (31)

However,

> belief is nothing but a more vivid, lively, forcible, firm, steady conception of an object, than what the imagination alone is ever able to attain. (32)

Thus belief about facts and the imagination of fictions arise from the same faculties of the mind, but differ in their relative intensity and "freedom."

A similar approach to the distinction between fact and fiction is used by J. R. R. Tolkien. Speaking specifically of the genre of fantasy, he defines it as a "sub-creation" by the imagination which rearranges and produces an alternative to "the Primary World" (67). Fantasy is a rational activity, seeking to produce "the inner consistency of reality" in a "Secondary World," in which one does believe while one is "in it" (60). Fantasy thus satisfies a primordial desire "to survey the depths of space and time" and "to hold communion with other living things" (44). It is the recovery of our original, human creative power (the image of God) which enables us to see things again "as we are (or were) meant to see them" (74).

Tolkien, as it were, inverts Hume. Where Hume sees fiction as weakened perception (and memory), Tolkien sees (at least one kind of) fiction as heightened and renewed perception. Both, however, see fiction in terms of the primacy of perception—for Hume, memory simply stores the perceived "ideas"—of actual objects. Fiction is a secondary, but more "free," association of ideas, units of sensory experience (cf. Sartre, n.d.:268–70).

Jeremy Bentham also distinguishes between real and fictitious entities.

> A fictitious entity is an entity to which, though by the

---

[4] For an approach to this same problem from a non-associationist perspective, see Jean-Paul Sartre, *The Psychology of Imagination*. Hector-Neri Castaneda distinguishes between the logic of the fictional copula (consociation) and that of the factual copula (consubstantiation) in "Fiction and Reality: Their Fundamental Connection": 34–39.

> grammatical form of the discourse employed in speaking of it, existence be ascribed, yet in truth and reality existence is not meant to be ascribed. . . . Every fictitious entity bears some relation to some real entity, and can no otherwise be understood than in so far as that relation is perceived—a conception of that relation is obtained. (12)

Fictions are not non-entities, but rather the necessary constructs of language, and in particular, of names. They are metaphors, analogies by which we speak of the real. Ambiguities inevitably arise when we mistakenly relate the real to the fictitious—e.g., as cause and effect. However, we cannot speak of the fictitious except as though it were real (60–61). Only in relation to the material is communication possible, and language thus arises as matter, and as a (fictional, elliptical) substitute for matter (64, 67).

> And thus it is by bringing to view other words, in the character of words of which, though not pronounced, the import was meant to be conveyed by the word which was pronounced, that a single word may be made to have the effect, and . . . comprise the import, of an indefinite number of other words . . . if nothing less than the import of an entire proposition be sufficient for the giving full expression to any the most simple thought, it follows that, no word being anything more than a fragment of a proposition, no word is of itself the complete sign of any thought. (68)

Thus, although Bentham does not draw the conclusion, language tends to fragment indefinitely. All language, he claims, is figurative (74). Written letters stand for spoken sounds, and the sounds stand for "ideas or other psychical entites, capable of being expressed by language" (107).[5] These ideas are real entities, as are the sense impressions of external objects.

A unifying thread running through these different approaches to the connection and difference between fact and fiction is the claim that fictionality does not lie in the content of the fictional statement (or other use of language), but rather in the way in which that statement is made. Therefore, analyzing the logical content of, e.g., a fictional christology will not give us its fictional quality. Instead, the fiction lies in the way in which the christology is stated—not a particular arrangement or type

---

[5] Cf. Aristotle, *On Interpretation*: 16a.

of words, but the conjunction of content and context, the referentiality of the statement. We see this quite clearly in Hume's
position, and Tolkien's analysis of the difference between Primary and Secondary as lying in creativity points to something
very similar (despite large differences in attitude). Both the Platonic and Aristotelian notions that (proper) *mimesis* requires that
the imitated reality take us to the ideal also suggest a manner of
conjunction. These theorists may not agree about what it is that
the fiction refers to, but they do agree that the difference
between fiction and fact lies in the reference. Bentham radi-
calizes the entire problem by asserting the fundamental fictionality of language itself. Within the essential referentiality of all
language there hides an unremovable fictionality.

We may return, then, to the claims of Gottlob Frege, which
were discussed in Chapter One. In his search for a pure conceptual notation, Frege finds a fundamental fault in language, in
sentences whose reference is in principle indeterminable.[6] These
sentences are not complete "statements," for they contain "functions"—places of potential variability in content—which remain
"unsaturated"*; in place of an "object," they give us only an
"empty sign" (31–32). They form divergent infinite series*
which cannot properly refer.

Functions, for Frege, are concepts, if they have one "empty
place" or point of non-saturation, and relations, if they have two
or more "empty places" (cf. Calloud: 19–20). They may also be
first-level, if potentially saturated (or "completed") by an object,
or second-level, if potentially saturated by a function (Frege: 39–
40). Therefore, a metaphor, conventionally conceived, is a relation between two concepts, one first-level (the "vehicle") and one
second-level (the "tenor").

A concept, unlike a name, is a predicate, according to Frege
(43). A concept may include a name, which refers to an object,[7]
and which may indeed be the name of another concept; this
would make the former concept second-level (e.g., the metaphor). Since a sentence links an object, the name of which forms

[6] Cf. Jacques Derrida's discussion of Husserl (1973:119–22).

[7] We must note again that "object," for Frege, excludes concepts and relations, but is otherwise used very broadly. "An object is anything that is not a
function, so that an expression for it does not contain any empty place" (32).
Both real and ideal objects would qualify here.

the grammatical subject, to a concept, which is the grammatical predicate, every sentence must contain at least one "empty place," or function; in order to form a thought (the sense, as the term was used in Chapter One), the sentence must be "completed" or "supplemented"—i.e. the "empty place" must be filled with an object (54). In other words, it must be made to refer.

However, if it should refer not to an object but to another sentence, or a part of a sentence containing an unsaturated function, then its emptiness cannot be filled until the reference of the second sentence (or phrase) is completed. This is where the threat of divergent infinite series appears, for this indirect reference suggests the possibility of an infinitely deferred reference, what we might call, extending Frege's terminology, a sentence containing an infinitely-leveled concept, which could never be properly supplemented, and which Frege identifies, as was noted in Chapter One, as metaphor, the "flaw" in language. We will consider metaphor, as a concept of infinitely-deferred reference, in Chapter Five.[8] We must remember here, however, Bentham's notion that language (and hence story) is essentially metaphorical.

Neither Frege nor Bentham is concerned explicitly with story. However, a number of recent literary theorists have adopted Frege's or similar approaches for their own use.

The phenomenologist Roman Ingarden locates the fictional objects of a literary work of art in neither the realm of the real (historical) nor that of the ideal, but in a realm which is determined by both.[9] Although he uses the terminology somewhat differently, Ingarden, like Frege, distinguishes between the "constants" of the content of the intended object and the "variables" of its concept (63–68). It is intentionality which separates the ontically autonomous—existing "on its own," real—from the ontically heteronomous—that which depends on another for its existence, fiction. As concepts, words have "stocks" of meaning which, depending upon their "actualization," may give rise to

---

[8] In light of Frege's analysis, what can we make of Maritain's metaphysical formula: "Every being is what it is"? This also would appear to be infinitely regressive, and therefore metaphorical. The poetic (message) and reference functions endlessly interchange with one another.

[9] Cf. Plato and Aristotle, discussed above. Ingarden's "third basis" of the literary work is the written letter—the hyletic phase of the sign (367). Again, his theory should be compared to Plato's.

multiple and ambiguous meanings (91). Sentences are intentionally formed according to "empty formal schema," and "the transformations in the individual word meanings appearing in the sentence, which go hand in hand with sentence-formation, are completely relative to the execution of this operation" (102; also 363). This intentionality determines every sentence as representing real or ideal objectivities (objects or states of affairs).

The intentionality of fiction determines its objectivities as "illusions"—that is, neither ontically transcendent nor non-existent—by "borrowing" from the intentionality of word meanings (123, 127). These fictions can be free and ambiguous in ways that real objectivities cannot; this Ingarden calls the "opalescent multiplicity"*of the fictional (142).

> Only the interweaving of unambiguous and ambiguous meaning elements brings about an ambiguous sentence. Correlatively, its purely intentional correlate content is constructed in such a way that it possesses a foundation of 'common' elements upon which the other elements, corresponding to the ambiguous expressions, are fastened in a remarkably multi-rayed manner. And they are only fastened, precisely because, between the unequivocally determined (the 'common') elements of the content and those belonging to the ambiguous expressions, there exists only a loose, not finally fixed, connection. (144)

The intending of the real is expressed in judgments (truth values) which are "rooted" in the ontically autonomous. In contrast, the fictional is intended in "quasi-judgments." Judgment supposes the identity of the cognition and the real; quasi-judgment simulates this supposition. The "quasi" of fiction modifies the propositional copula—the "is" of "S is P"—so that it neither asserts (of reality) nor is neutral.[10] Just as there are a potentially infinite number of levels of functions for Frege, so there are a potentially infinite number of "quasi"-levels (182). It is because of this that stories can form a world—however, not a

---

[10] Again, cf. H.-N. Castaneda's discussion of the fictional copula. Also see Husserl (section 114); Derrida, 1973 (chapter 4); Bachelard, 1969:29; Sartre, n.d.:13. William James distinguishes between fiction, as solipsism, and fact, as that mediation through which subjectivities may operate on one another, in "The Function of Cognition" (1909). However, his distinction depends on a further distinction between a story itself and any specific version or instance of the story, which he identifies with the author's intention.

"serious" one. The fiction "substitutes" for the real (171), and therefore it always has a doubleness of content and context which the real does not. On the other hand, objects in reality possess an infinite manifold of properties, contents, "sides," etc., but fictional objects are composed of a finite selection of "states of affairs," although a potentially infinite "stock" may be co-intended. In contrast to the "unequivocally determined," absolutely unique, real object, the fictional object contains "spots of indeterminacy"* and is composed of inevitably general determinants.[11] Fictional representation both reveals and conceals the object—conceals its finitude, its fictionality.

> We can say that, with regard to the determination of the objectivities represented within it, every literary work is in principle incomplete and always in need of further supplementation; in terms of the text, however, this supplementation can never be completed. (251)

This incompleteness demands a "completion" in the act of reading and makes possible the polysemy of the story. Not only is fiction freed from the empirical restraints of the factual, but its incompleteness establishes a "duality" or disequilibrium within the represented object which breaks down its identity and the self-identity of the entire representation. In reading, this incompleteness is overlooked and "supplemented," so that an illusion—one of many possible ones—of (complete) reality appears. These are the "concretizations"*of the literary work of art, variations which are possible because of its schematic formation (cf. Sartre, n.d.:48). Because they arise in the reading, these concretizations "go beyond" the work itself and become a means by which it is "violated" (Ingarden: 353). However, if the ideal substructures of the work are substantially changed, the metaphysics of the work is transformed and it changes or loses identity. Without the concretization the work is "nothing"; through it, the story "suffer[s] defenselessly all our operations" and becomes an "incarnation" (372–73).

The structuralist Roman Jakobson describes the poetic function of language as concerned primarily with the "message" (= content, sense) of statements. Like all of the six language functions, the poetic function plays a greater or lesser part in every instance

[11] Cf. Castaneda's discussion of "thin thinkable individuals" (26–32). Also Calloud: 42; Sartre, n.d.:11, 189.

of language, but it predominates in poetry (cf. Wellek/Warren: 12, 15). The operation of the poetic function consists in the transference of what Jakobson calls "equivalence"*—the "space-logic" of Joseph Frank—from the paradigmatic (selection) axis of language to the syntagmatic (combination) axis.

> In poetry one syllable is equalized with any other syllable of the same sequence; word stress is assumed to equal word stress, as unstress equals unstress; prosodic long is matched with long, and short with short; word boundary equals word boundary, no boundary equals no boundary; syntactic pause equals syntactic pause, no pause equals no pause. (Jakobson: 358; cf. Calloud: 43.)

The poetic function focuses upon the message itself as linguistic phenomenon, establishing an equality or parallelism among the units.

> In poetry not only the phonological sequence but in the same way any sequence of semantic units strives to build an equation. Similarity superimposed on contiguity imparts to poetry its thoroughgoing symbolic, multiplex, polysemantic essence. . . . Said more technically, anything sequent is a simile. (Jakobson: 370)

This establishes an ambiguity: the poetry is "quasi-quoted" and its reference is "split."[12] On the one hand, it refers to the reality of a world (the reference to which the sense should properly point, in Frege's view); on the other hand, it refers to itself as message (the indirect reference to a concept, an unsaturated function, which is itself, setting up an infinite regression). It appears to be simultaneously a first- and a second-level concept. This repetitive self-referentiality* makes the poetic reiterable; or as Joseph Frank has said, in a not-very-different context, the literary work is always re-read (1963:19).[13] There is a disruption of the direct referentiality between signifier and signified, demanding a continual re-reading. For Jakobson, as for Ingarden, the ambiguity of the poetic function draws heavily

---

[12] The close relation between Jakobson's poetic theory and Lévi-Strauss's analysis of myth must be noted (Lévi-Strauss: 62–65). Also, cf. Castaneda's notion of "story-operators" (19ff.). However, story-operators appear to be either historical authors or the more general "people say" or "it is said." This tends to resolve inappropriately the ambiguity of the fictional frame.

[13] Cf. Derrida, 1973:155–56; Husserl: 287 (sections 111, 112).

upon, and is inconceivable without, the materiality of the sign, which belongs to two other functions (cf. Ingarden: one other stratum) of the linguistic phenomenon: the contact (phatic) and the code (metalingual) functions.

Prose tends to be more referential and less poetic than verse, according to Jakobson (374). However, even in prose there is no escaping from referential ambiguity, at least in those prose forms most dominated by the poetic function. (Ingarden and Bentham regard their theories of fiction as applying in various ways to all language, including non-fictional discourse such as scientific reports.)

Jakobson's theory of split reference has been of particular importance to Paul Ricoeur, who has drawn upon it for both a theory of narrative (1978b) and one of metaphor (1976, 1978a). For Ricoeur, fictional narrative is fundamentally metaphoric in its split referentiality, or as I have called it, self-referentiality (1978a:152–53). According to Ricoeur, it is precisely this which distinguishes fictional narratives from factual (historical) ones, in which proper referentiality—truth-claims, evidence, etc.—predominates.

He argues that a totally "self-contained" literature—e.g., the works of spatial form, which Frank has described—consisting of works which refer only to themselves and which therefore establish an extreme limit to fictional ambiguity, results from the disruption of the referentiality of language by writing (1976:33). He sees a possible conflict between Jakobson's theory of split reference and the distinction between the poetic and referential functions (1978b:199, n. 5); this limits Ricoeur's theory of metaphor, as we shall see in Chapter Five. It also results in his distinction between the historical and the fictional; for Ricoeur, history (as facts) is prior to story, and reference is prior to split reference (1978b:196). I have argued in the first two chapters that self-referentiality in such a pure form is impossible (or unrecognizable); the other extreme, the pure referentiality of a complete congruity of signifier and signified, is likewise impossible. Both fictional and factual (historical) narratives lie within the self-referential ambiguity of the frames of story, and thus all story is fundamentally fictional. Fiction and fact are to be distinguished not in terms of material components of the story—the sign, which inevitably grounds the ambiguity—but in terms of an "external," "non-material" component, namely, the subjective apprehension of the story, or belief.[14]

3. Belief

To be sure, at least some stories have ways of telling us that they are fictional—"this is only a story," "once upon a time . . . ," etc.—or that they are factual—"this is a true story," "on June 12, 1944, it happened that . . . ," etc. The "artificiality" of verse as opposed to the "naturalness" of prose may also suggest such a distinction, as may numerous other indicators—e.g., footnotes, special uses of verb tenses, types of titles, etc. We do not normally begin stories with "This is a false story." To do so is either to place it within a clinical setting—a larger story—or so to disrupt it as to threaten its identity as a story. These are part (or some) of the frames of story, and as such they all—not just the indicators of fact—may be undercut by the disruption between content and context.

Ricoeur is not the only one attempting to clarify (and justify) the conventional distinction between fact and fiction. We are reminded of Hume's distinction between ("belief" in) facts and fiction as resting in a difference of intensity based upon the conjunction of sensory data. Frege places beliefs (and doubts) among statements containing second-level functions. Ingarden goes to considerable lengths to argue that the distinction is not a problem, although his argument concludes that the problem is more epistemological—in the apprehension of the story—than ontological—in the structure of the story as an object of consciousness (173–81). Jakobson demonstrates how the process of quotation transforms fact into assertion of belief, eliminating the possibility of truth-values (377–78).

Yet in all of these approaches, we see—in some, more clearly than in others—an unresolvable ambiguity underlying language itself (and story in particular) and undercutting all efforts toward a clear referentiality. If we agree with Ricoeur (and Ingarden, and Frege) that factual claims, and indeed any sort of scientific, objective language, demand this sort of clear, direct referentiality, then we must also see (with Ingarden and

---

[14] Scholes and Kellogg argue that "history" and fiction emerge historically as alternatives from the breakdown of the ancient traditional authority of narratives (chapter 7). Cf. also H. R. Jauss: 597–98. This, however, concerns the history of genres, not the metaphysics of story.

Bentham, at least) that the possibility of this sort of language rests upon a prior fictionality, which we have already suggested in the preceding and shall further develop as the infinitely undecidable self-referentiality of language.[15] Story, therefore, does tend to be propositional, but its propositions are inevitably incomplete, and they must be completed by belief.

Fact emerges from a prior fictionality through what we here call belief. It should be clear that this term is not here restricted to religious belief, although that is included. Belief applies to neither the logically impossible—despite Alice's friend, the White Queen—nor the logically necessary, but to that which is contingent and thus factual. If the logical necessity of God could be demonstrated, then belief in God would become impossible for any rational person. Belief therefore cannot be demonstrated with certainty, except in terms of some other, already assumed belief. It is beyond reason, but essential to thought. Belief is closely related to what Kant calls "judgment" (whether aesthetic or reflective), as that which seeks to bring the contingent into conformity with the necessary (20).

Belief appears in story in the tension or dialectic—the "ironic gap" (Scholes/Kellogg: 256)—between what I have previously called the "beholder" and what Wayne Booth has called the "implied dialogue"* of the narrative (155). This dialogue is the circuit of communication between an implied author* and a postulated reader ("implied reader"*: Chatman), who do not (usually) actually appear as characters in the story but serve as the poles which make the narrative as such possible. Thus the actual (real) narrating does not occur directly between a real teller and a real audience, but only indirectly through these narrative structures, which are "masks" or "roles" that author and reader must wear or play.[16] Booth argues that these structures are both created by the author; this seems to me to assert the primacy of the historical-critical method and the metaphysical separation—each with its own identity—of author and reader. It would be better to say that author and reader are established by the story, in the intentional act of selection which gives it a meaning—the same intentional act which establishes my own real self as the "author" and/or "reader" of "this story."

15 See Husserl: 184 (section 70); cf. Derrida, 1973.
16 Cf. Sartre, n.d.:250–51; Bachelard, 1969:13.

This act of selection necessarily involves both intellectual and emotional elements.

This is the "quasi-quoted" aspect of story noted by Jakobson, Ingarden, and others (cf. also Frege: 65). Because of its essential ambiguity, the reader as much as the author "creates" the work; this is the work of genre, a framing which "ignores" the incompleteness by covering it over or regarding it as trivial, and which suppresses the referential ambiguity by deciding the nature of the work. As Booth suggests, the story requires a contract between reader and author (52–53), a contract which takes the form of the implied dialogue. However, it is the contract which makes us what we are: my wedding vows make me a husband, my mortgage makes me a landowner, etc. These are precisely the "facts" of my existence; even the factual notation of my weight and height requires accepted conventions or "contracts" (cf. Scholes, 1974:108–9).

The relation between implied dialogue and beholder is complex. The story appears as both "mine"—that which I have produced, by writing and/or reading, to which I have committed myself—and yet also as "other"—over which I do not have complete control, which continually "escapes" me. To be sure, as author I can stop writing, and as reader I can stop reading. Nonetheless, as reader I am in the author's hands, and as author I am in the reader's hands (cf. Scholes/Kellogg: 275). The story is always both much more and much less than the meaning that I give to it, as I discover upon re-reading it, or discussing its meaning with others. Does it overflow with meaning, or is it so lacking in meaning that it must submit passively to the meanings which I inflict upon it? The intentional act which selects a story and gives it meaning, thereby giving an identity to myself and an identity to the world of the story, is belief.

We cannot examine at length here the widely-used phrase, "suspension of disbelief," as applied to fiction. I. A. Richards distinguishes two types of belief—emotional and intellectual—which pertain to the reading of poetry (1929:272ff.). These beliefs interfere with the reading, according to Richards, if the author's and reader's respective positions conflict either logically or emotively. Richards, however, supposes that the author's beliefs are somehow "in" the work; it would be better to say that the contract which is the work establishes a common basis of belief, just as it identifies author and reader. The contract, by providing the way in which the work is believed, is the work of genre.

To be sure, if we classify a story as "fiction," we say in a sense, "I don't believe it," and to the extent that we continue to read it, we withhold that disbelief. We do not, strictly speaking, disbelieve, nor are we ever indifferent as to belief. There may, however, be a sort of pre-belief, such as what Gaston Bachelard has called "reverie," in which

> one can know states which are ontologically below being and above nothingness. In these states the contradiction between being and non-being fades away. A sub-being (*moins-être*) is trying itself out as being. This antecedence of being does not yet have the responsibility of being. Neither does it have the solidity of the constituted being which believes itself capable of confronting a non-being. In such a state of mind, one feels clearly that logical opposition, with its too bright light, erases all possibility of penumbral ontology. (1969:111)

At such points, we encounter as nearly as possible the self-referential ambiguity of the work, not in the work itself, but in our own imagination—we escape briefly from our self-identity. However, to dwell permanently in such a state would be madness, and our need for identity soon returns us to the realm of the metaphysical; our free reverie on the story returns to the safety of the hermeneutical enclosure of genre.

> The essential ambiguity of the unreal object appears to us to be one of the main factors of the fear of imagination. A clear and distinct perception is . . . eminently reassuring. . . . This *suspicious* character is the reason why an imaginary object is never fully itself. (Sartre, n.d.:189; emphasis Sartre's)

Reading (and of course writing) inevitably require a commitment or risking of the self, a going out of one's self in order to further "appropriate" one's self. The concreteness of existence seeks expression in the dangerous fictionality of language.

Belief "clarifies" the relation between beholder and story by establishing a meaning. It negates the original negativity of referential ambiguity, thereby producing a positivity. In resolving the identity of the story, it suppresses the ambiguity of self-referentiality (split reference), with more or less success. We have already noted the part played by the hyletic* material of the sign in this dialectic: we might even speak of the essential unbelief of the word. Belief forgets the sign and tends to establish unambiguous referentiality as the identity of the story.[17]

The nature of this identity and its appropriate referentiality is determined by genre, the metaphysics of which will be examined in Chapter Four. Let us note in a preliminary way, however, that we call those stories "fictional" which tend to escape, in various ways, from the demands of belief, in which the tension between beholder and implied dialogue is too great to permit a convincing illusion of direct reference. This is the "suspension" of reference which Frank sees as arising from the spatial juxtaposition of the meaning-elements of the story. Spatial form is thus more "fictional"—more resistant to belief—than temporal form; or—again following Worringer's lead—it demands a belief in a world radically other than the empirical world of ordinary experience. For example, the influence of cubism on Lagerkvist, and his hostility to naturalism, have been widely noted. Naturalism, for Lagerkvist, turns "fiction" into a "lie."[18] We also noted, in Chapter Two, the affinities of spatial form with myth. The juxtapositions in the story demand juxtapositions on the part of the beholder—beliefs—which refer the story to an ideal or abstract ("philosophical") order.

On the other hand, "factual" stories are "captured" by our belief, and the tension is kept well under control. Fact appears as the reflection of an external reality, a reality ultimately independent of our subjective intentionality. This is the way taken by empirical science, and it is determined in the metaphysics of the scientific method. However, the difference between fact and fiction may as well be said to lie in the personal, cultural, and other contexts of our belief as in the story itself; they are opposite sides of the same thing. Thus belief not only forgets the sign but it forgets story itself and projects a world and a self as distinct entities. In both fiction and fact—as the object of belief— what Jakobson calls the poetic function, or rather, the oscillation between the poetic and the referential, is suppressed; each one negates the original negativity or fictionality (metaphoricity) of story as language.

We can now return to the end of part one of this chapter,

---

[17] Cf. Derrida, 1973:56; Sartre, n.d.:16, 91, 166.
[18] Cf. Spector (18–20, 78), Kort (32–34), Lagerkvist (Buckman: 19–21).

and the observation that christological fantasies would appear to be heresies, were they not regarded as fictions. Borges even introduces the fictitious theologian of "Three Versions of Judas" to us as a potential heresiarch and states that he would have been much more comfortable among the Gnostics than as a modern biblical scholar. He is an "ascetic of the spirit," seeking to avoid the "fallacy of time." Anthony Kerrigan, the translator of Borges's story, describes Borges himself as a "vindicator of heresies," and he quotes Unamuno to the effect that heresy is necessary to theology. "And exegesis is the mother of heresy" (Kerrigan in Borges: 10).

It is probably over-simplistic, but at least somewhat accurate, to say that theology begins as heresy, as that which asks the uncomfortable questions, seeking absolute consistency and clarity, regardless of the expense. Heresy exposes the logical incongruities of the mythically ideal realm, the undecidability which has been suppressed by the religious myth, and it demands, in effect, a re-writing or supplementation of the myth—a re-reading. Only when it becomes evident that the heretical questions and the demand for rationality cannot be ignored is there an attempt to establish a compromise position, in order to "save" the myth, which is orthodoxy. If orthodoxy is such a compromise, it is between the heretical demand for absolute rationality and the need for metaphysical identity and stability, which is expressed in myth.

Such a conjecture does fit the christological fantasies discussed above. If the fictional beliefs of Barabbas and the sibyl are heretical (or "quasi-heretical"), it is because they display too clearly the fundamental ambiguities of, in Barabbas's case, Christianity, and in the sibyl's case, religion in general (and especially "nature-religions"). Ahasuerus's beliefs stand somewhere between those of Barabbas and the sibyl, but they likewise express a fundamental ambiguity. The fictional formulators of these christologies are driven to make sense of experience and knowledge which exceed their grasp. For each character, the myth has "come apart," through direct contact with the inscrutable, morally ambiguous divinity. Each one lives in a chaos which he or she cannot tolerate, which demands to be organized, a puzzle with pieces that do not fit and which thereby become an obsession. The demand for understanding triumphs, and it frequently leads to the character's destruction.

It seems odd today to speak of heresy and orthodoxy; we are more comfortable with terms such as pluralism and relativism. If, however, heresy is the source of theology, then the modern malaise of systematic theology may be explained as a lack of good heresies. Theology—and contemporary thought in general—is too quick to grasp at stories, to seek a univocal meaning, an identity, and a reassuringly teleological linear temporality. Theology needs exegetical heresy to "infect" thought with new ideas, so that understanding may grow through the struggle with them. On the other hand, if literature (fiction) can serve as a sort of heretical source, then this may explain the attractiveness of literary studies to some theologians. If orthodoxy is a compromise between heresies, or between the extreme rationality of heresy and the fundamental, metaphysical need for identity, then orthodoxy may be seen as a particular variety of heresy, and by analogy, what we call "fact" is a particular variety of fiction.[19]

If we accept this argument, then we have specified the genus of fact as fiction, but we have still not specified its proper difference: what distinguishes facts from other fictions? Why and how are we able to suppress the self-referentiality of some stories so easily, while others seem to escape us endlessly? Why does the separation between fact and fiction—here minimized—seem so obvious, and the connection between them—here emphasized—seem so obscure?

It is in connection with questions such as these that it may be helpful to conceive the difference between facts and other fictions as a difference between genres. We are all aware that characters, plots, etc. undergo specifiable transformations when they are transplanted (or better, when they "migrate," as Hector-Neri Castaneda says) from one literary form to another—from the epic poem to the drama or the novel, etc.—or even from one work to another, yet they retain some identifiable continuity, even though represented by different artists in different eras.[20]

---

[19] Cf. Husserl: 134 (section 47), 206 (section 79); James, "The Function of Cognition."

[20] Ingarden also discusses this phenomenon. Cf. Ziolkowski: 6–8, 49–53; also see John S. Dunne's comments on the relativity of standpoints, and on understanding the story as story.

If facts are a genre or set of genres, then transplanting a christology from a Borges story or a Lagerkvist novel or some other work will not be impossible or even unlikely, but it will not happen without transformation of the fiction, either. Consider all that Nietzsche, Camus, and others have said about human existence as "acting;" practice turns fiction into fact. If I should choose tomorrow to become the sibyl of Lagerkvist's story, then she would cease to be ("only") a fiction and would become a fact, insofar as I was able to incarnate her.[21] Likewise, the sibyl's fictional christology becomes factual the moment that some existing mind comes to precisely the same conclusion; yet it will not be the same conclusion, because it will have been violated and transformed in ways determined by laws of the transplanting of entities between genres.

What sorts of transformations do real persons, ideas, events, etc. undergo when they are introduced into fictional works, and what laws govern these transformations? If orthodoxy is a compromised and controlled form of heresy, where then lies the compromise or control that turns fiction into fact? We can answer these questions if the nature of the genre(s) of fact can be specified, as the nature of literary genres can be specified, with some accuracy. What would a generic, or literary, analysis of reality—both factual and fictional—look like, and how would it draw upon, or be determined by, metaphysics?

[21] Note the "startling case" which Castaneda cites; also, James's example of the dream (214).

Chapter Four
GENRE AND REALITY

If "story" is to replace metaphysics, as numerous contemporary thinkers in theology, ethics, and other areas suggest, then we must uncover the metaphysics of story. If we are using a concept of story which contains a hidden metaphysical core, then we have not at all avoided the ambiguities of metaphysics, nor have we escaped from metaphysics into some freer, more enlightened space, but we have simply deluded ourselves. We may have introduced a new wrinkle into the traditional philosophical strategies, but in the long run, we have not saved ourselves from anything (in any sense of the word "save"), and we must sooner or later return to the "dreary work" of systematic metaphysics.

Therefore, the metaphysics of the distinction between fact and fiction must be exposed, insofar as these terms are applied to stories, including stories about reality. It was suggested in the previous chapter that this distinction is not absolute, but rather on the order of a distinction between genres in literature; in other words, what is conventionally termed a "fact" is one type (or set of types) of fictional story, of which what are usually called "fictions" are other types. However, all stories, as phenomena of language, contain and suppress to a greater or lesser degree a fundamental fictionality, which I have called self-referentiality.* This means that the metaphysics of genre must also be uncovered.

The term "metaphysics" eludes an easy or simple definition; however, in general it refers to some understanding of absolute or ultimate reality, to whatever explains why there is a world—and a self in relation to it—and why the world is the way it is. The history of philosophy has witnessed many varying attempts to describe this reality, e.g., in terms of substance, form, process, event, etc. Perhaps the common characteristic of all of these attempts is the longing for totality, for completeness or a sense of unity, the search for a fundamental principle in terms of which all questions can finally be answered, for a ground upon/within which we can rest secure. In Chapter One, we noted the principle of identity, which according to Maritain underlies all metaphysics, and which finds ancient expression in the Parmenidean sphere, to which Heidegger has more recently (and controversially) referred.

This is not intended to be a comprehensive survey of genre theory.[1] Nor does this chapter explore specific generic typologies. What it attempts is to isolate some basic conceptions of genre, and to engage in an analysis which could be applied to any other theory. Nor are all of the theories here considered explicitly genre theories; Wittgenstein does not refer to genre at all, and Gadamer and Güttgemanns do so only in passing, and vaguely. In these cases, it is suggested that there are implicit in their works genre theories, or perspectives upon genre theory, which must be considered. In other words, these works throw light upon the metaphysics of genre.

These theories have been divided somewhat arbitrarily into two groups or approaches to genre, according to the ways in which they utilize the "hermeneutical circle." This term is probably overused; nonetheless, the framework described by it does persist throughout all genre theories, and it expresses in a fundamental way the metaphysics of genre. It is commonly described as the mutual dependence, for understanding, of the part and the whole. How can I know the part (any object of knowledge, or more specifically, a work of literature) if I do not know the whole of which it is the part (the genre); yet how can I know the whole except as the sum of its parts? How can I understand unless I already understand? What appears superficially to be an insoluble problem is actually a very useful heuristic instrument, which plays an important role, e.g., in the classical Aristotelian method of definition by genus and difference. This logical method, as its name implies, is very closely related to literary genre theory, as well as to other classificatory systems. Although literary theorists frequently downplay the similarity between genres and other systems (biological species, chemical elements, etc.) by noting that genres can change quite suddenly, while the

---

[1] Paul Hernadi surveys a great many contemporary genre theories in his book, *Beyond Genre*. Cf. also the journal *Poetics*, 10:2/3 (June, 1981).

other sorts of classifications change only very slowly, or not at all (numbers, geometrical shapes), this distinction does not seem to be a very important one, as the fundamental nature of this relationship between part and whole is a logical, and not a historical, one. Genre tends to be synchronic, but unless we take it to be a Platonic, eternal form, there will also be a diachronic dynamics to it.[2] But here already are the beginnings of a problem of genre theory.

The two ways in which the hermeneutical circle are used[3] in genre theory are what will be called here the circle of pragmatics and the circle of semantics. These terms are borrowed from semiotic theory, but without necessarily confining their meaning to the semiological usage. The two circles correspond roughly to the distinction which operates in the two central chapters of Paul Hernadi's book, between theories which center upon the auther and reader, and those which focus upon the structure of the work and its representation of a world. Theories which are oriented upon the circle of pragmatics concern themselves with genre as a vehicle of understanding or communication between two positions, which are normally thought of as minds or rational subjects (cf. Scholes: 130). Thus this circle concerns the question of belief, as described in Chapter Three, the relation between the beholder and the implied dialogue of the story, in which (to use Frege's terms) its sense is completed by a reference. Theories which are oriented upon the circle of semantics are concerned with genre as a coherence of units of language within the work which is simultaneously a correspondence with units of meaning which both define the genre and constitute a world. This circle concerns the "deeper" level of the ambiguity between (in Frege's terms) sign and sense, the problem of the generation of meaning from meaningless material objects (letters, sounds).

---

[2] T. S. Eliot's "Tradition and the Individual Talent" is perhaps the best-known statement of the historical dimension of genre. Cf. Crossan, 1973:16–18; Heidegger (on Wilhelm von Humboldt), 1971a:136; Jakobson: 352.

[3] There are other ways to understand this circle: Socrates's method of dialectic, Anselm's formulation of "faith seeking understanding," and Kant's analysis of the discord between reason and imagination; cf. also Girard: 240; Heidegger, 1971a:51.

1. The Circle of Pragmatics

E. D. Hirsch, Jr. is perhaps the best-known and most force-ful proponent of this approach. He defines genre as follows:

> It is that sense of the whole by means of which an inter-preter can correctly understand any part of its deter-minacy . . . this determining sense of the whole is not identical with the particular meaning of the utterance. That particular meaning arises when the generic expec-tations have been fulfilled in a particular way by a par-ticular sequence of words. (1967:86)

A genre is a system of social conventions, analogous to what Wittgenstein calls "language-games," a type which enables the communication of meaning because it establishes a set of expec-tations. The genre itself is not the meaning, but a type or "con-trolling idea" which is a structure into which word sequences may fit (79). Genre lies between language (*langue*) and actual speech (*parole*) as a convenience, a heuristic concept which when applied correctly produces understanding.

For Ludwig Wittgenstein, language-games are "forms of life" which make sentences (structures of meaning) possible (par. 19–20). Games evolve and change historically; there are new games and old games. These games consist of rules, which unite the parts and the whole. It is the rules which enable two people to play the game, and to communicate. The rules establish an order, which enables one to anticipate what is going to come next (par. 187–88). Interpretation (including reading) is a derivation of meaning according to the appropriate rules; it does not create the meaning but only determines it according to the customary rules (par. 198–99; Sartre, n.d.:243), Language therefore "carries" meaning. The text is like a puzzle or labyrinth to be solved. "It is in language that an expectation and its fulfillment make contact" (par. 445). It is the possibility of common experience.

The rules of a language-game are its grammar, which makes possible the representation of objects and the expression of "essences" (par. 371). Grammar itself is arbitrary, purely conven-tional. There is no intrinsic relation between different language-games; there are only "families of resemblances." Each game has its own "point," which defines what is essential and unessential to it (par. 564). Interpretation is thus a sort of hypothesis-formation—Ricoeur calls it a "guess"—which if correct is verified within the game. Meaning is not a hidden, subjective process, but simply the identification and playing of a particular language-game according to its appropriate rules. Purely personal or private thoughts or ideas cannot be communicated at all, but only that which can be intended according to the rules of a game. Wittgenstein at this point sounds very much like Frege, and what the rules permit is what Frege calls "sense." Is the genre-game then a second-level function*?

Hans-Georg Gadamer is another major source of Hirsch's thought. Gadamer's explicit mention of genre is brief, but it leads immediately into his phenomenology of interpretation. Genre is closely related to style and manner, according to Gadamer, and therefore it is a normative unity of expression, an expression of an historical attitude and structure; the classical is the climax of the life of a genre (1975:257). Questions of genre therefore focus on the relation between creation and imitation, which reflects the hermeneutical dialectic of part and whole. How can a genre, as a pattern that is repeatable and repeated, incorporate that which is new—not a repetition? Gadamer understands this dialectic in terms of play, which is "free creation" (171). Play is the self-representation of a meaningful whole, the presentation of true being in a "closed circle of meaning" (101). Play has rules which establish a spatial structure (a world) and permit its repetition. Play reveals the essence of things; it allows us to recognize the possibilities of being, yet within a tradition (a canon). It therefore both creates and re-creates. It establishes a continuity which is prior to any imaginative disruption, and which permits a repetition that is the same (as previous occurrences) and yet historically distinct, different (106–11).[4] It thus establishes presence as *theoria*—sharing, self-forgetfulness—as ecstasy and event (in the Heideggerian sense of those words).

Language for Gadamer is conventional. It is, however, also an "infinite dialogue" which approaches the limits of expression and understanding (493). It is the attempt to achieve mastery over reality, and thus it forms the core of rationality. Writing is self-alienation, and it must be re-appropriated through hermeneutics, which is the intention of wholeness, the reviving of the "dead trace of meaning" (146).

[4] Both Wittgenstein and Gadamer should be compared to Johann Huizinga's theory of play in *Homo Ludens*.

Play relates to literary theory in terms of the question of reading. Reading is the hermeneutical play that completes the text. It is a dialectic of object (text) and project (reader) which culminates in a "fusing of horizons,"* an intentional act of translation/interpretation involving re-creation and renunciation (273, 348). The intentionality of what we have called the beholder is identified with the implied dialogue* of the work. This fusing is accomplished through the hermeneutical circle of question and answer leading to a "common statement."

> . . . it is always, in whatever tradition we consider it, a human, i.e. a linguistically constituted world, that presents itself to us. Every such world, as linguistically constituted, is always open, of itself, to every possible insight and hence for every expansion of its own world-picture, and accordingly available to others. (405)

Hermeneutics presupposes the completeness of truth, and it seeks within its circles the objective validity of the text and of history, according to Gadamer. Genre integrates strangeness and familiarity in the play of a universal function which comprises all objects (365). Objective validity in interpretation is also the goal of Hirsch. He admits, with Gadamer (and Wittgenstein and Frege), that the goal is not to establish somehow the subjective state or interior consciousness of the author, and that even if that could be established it might not be important—the same would also apply to the individual reader—but he does insist upon the notion of a valid interpretation, the discovery of the "intrinsic genre," which can be clearly distinguished from the invalid, "extrinsic genre," in terms of what Hirsch calls a "willed type," or what Gadamer calls the horizon of the work (Hirsch: 88, 124). Genre, although a convention, is nonetheless the revelation of being in and across history.

If genres, as Hirsch uses the term, are kinds of language-games, then several observations can be made. First, this is an essentially nominalistic theory. Genres are the products of social convention. They are born and die within history. This theory does not readily account, however, for meaningful changes within genre; indeed, if the rules are subject to change, then the likelihood of confusion and misunderstanding is increased. How can the rules be changed historically, and what effect do the changes have on the game?

Second, and arising from the first observation, the theory has difficulty with the question of creativity and novelty. How can this genre theory account for the understanding of works which do not fit readily into a given language-game: for example, a work which lies in between two genres, or one which seriously distorts the rules of a genre? Hirsch notes that it is only in terms of the genre as type that the similarities and differences of the individual work may be identified. Genre is not a narrow concept, but a range of traits or "implications" reminiscent of Wittgenstein's "family resemblances" (Hirsch: 67–70). Each of these implications is in turn a sub-type with implications of its own; these establish a "structure of expectations," explicit and implicit, in terms of which the new phenomenon may be identified through "metaphorical* assimilation" (108). This is the play of which Gadamer speaks. Genre is a unifying ground, a horizon in terms of which the particular individuality of the work may be seen (Hirsch: 272).

This suggests a third observation, which concerns the difficulty that this theory has with the question of translation. If the work is understood as a meaning which can be communicated—Frege's "sense," the possibility of an objectively valid interpretation—does this give it an identity which can then be translated or transferred into another language or language-game? Wittgenstein is undecided; the question, for him, is whether or not the thought can be separated from the words expressing it (par. 531). This is also Frege's position. If they can be separated, the statement is a proposition; if not, it is a poem. The first can be translated and the second cannot.

Finally, this theory separates genre from literature. Genre is the point which makes possible the game and determines the essential, and although the point may not be achieved in any other way than through the game, the point is nevertheless not the same as the game; it is in a sense the end of the game.[5] Genre is teleological.

---

[5] This "point" would appear to be the same as Frege's notion of sense. Sense, however, is conceptual; in contrast, note Heidegger's remarks on the "end" of philosophy (1972:55ff.).

2. The Circle of Semantics

One must not draw too sharp a line between the two hermeneutical circles. The possibility of communication or understanding between author and reader raises the question of the relation
between text and paradigmatic units of meaning, and vice versa.
As we noted in Chapter One, the questions of value and canon,
although at the "opposite limits" of story, nonetheless come very
close to one another at certain points. However, the distinction
between the circles is not unimportant. In the first case, the
problem is primarily one of history; in the second case, it is primarily one of logic.

The genre theory of Northrop Frye is also well-known.
Although he uses the term "genre" only for portions of his general theory of literature, the entire theory seems pertinent to the
present study. For Frye, genre is an intermediate form between
the super-generic categories of narrative, which are arranged in
the mythic cyclicality of romantic/tragic/ironic/comic, in opposed pairs (1957:162). These categories establish archetypal
forms, which are (again) social conventions that assimilate
images and shape literature. There are four genres: the three
Platonic ones (drama, lyric, epic), plus prose fiction. Genre is the
"radical of presentation," an analogous form or correspondence
of order between works, through which that which was latent
may become manifest (246, 97). In addition, there are five
"modes" of fictional narration, arranged in hierarchical order:
the mythic, the romantic, the high mimetic, the low mimetic,
and the ironic (33). The coherence between these archetypes,
genres, and modes is not clear, and it is controversial. Todorov,
for example, criticizes Frye's incoherence severely (1973:12), as
does Scholes (1974:118ff.).

What does seem clear, however, is that literature for Frye is
essentially mythic, that myth is essentially fictional—that is,
made for its own sake, a "game"—and that this mythical fiction
is prior to the everyday world of historical fact, in the sense that
that world is meaningless without the mythic framework. Genre,
then, serves the function of mediating between this framework
and empirical existence; it is a function of what I have called
"belief." Genre functions as a set of conventional rules, established by a social-historical context, by which story regulates
itself, and which reflects a conceptual "unseen center" (1963a:

11). For Frye, the interplay between the historical/genealogical and the structural/synchronic is complex and ambiguous. Myth tells us of the gods, which are artifacts indicating the limits of the human. Myth is cosmological; it establishes a unified, whole world, not through logic, but through metaphor (31–32, 57). It is therefore both meta-historical and metaphysical. Genre bridges the gap between the myth and the actual work of literature, permitting a recognition (*anagnorisis*) in the order of words, of the way things are. Frye even suggests that there are non-literary genres: conceptual/rhetorical categories which function in a manner analogous to genre outside of the realm of literature (1957:329).[6]

Tzvetan Todorov develops his genre theory as a critical response to Frye's theory. Todorov claims that he wants to develop a scientific method for the study of literature, in which genre will serve as an "operative principle" (1973:3). Again, genre is an intermediate level of generality between literature as a whole and the individual work. Genre is a sub-group united by certain common properties dictating the transformation of the system of language. Here the circle is explicitly between the individual work of literature (*parole*) and the literary possibilities within language (*langue*). Todorov notes that language is intrinsically generic; it is impossible to say anything without saying it in a generic form, since all words are universals (1973:7). Wittgenstein makes a similar point. Genre functions as a relay, and a norm; it is a system of discourse.

Genres are constructions, principles of classification dictating the properties of the work and its law, according to Todorov. He notes, in relation to Frye's classification system, that there are logical "holes" in it, points where one might reasonably expect a genre to be formed, but where as yet none exists. On this basis, he distinguishes between historical genres and theoretical genres—genres which are logically, formally possible, but which do not yet have any instances (13). Genre is therefore a fundamentally logical, synchronic set of categories, which are incarnated contingently and historically. They are historical transformations of logical/universal grammar (1977:225).

The chief task of genre, and its chief problem, according to Todorov, is the relationship to novelty. How are works which do

[6] Hernadi's generic classifications, and his discussion of them, also imply this.

not abide by current generic laws to be accounted for? He uses this question to establish a distinction between popular and serious art (including literature). Popular genres (e.g., the detective story) are characterized by a refusal to admit of any variations or transformations of generic structure; in contrast, genres of a more seriously artistic type are continually being transformed and evolving. The characteristic of the great work of art is that it transforms the genre, or in some cases, creates a previously unknown genre.[7] This position seems diametrically opposed to Gadamer's discussion of the classic, as noted above. According to Todorov, genre is a center of arrangement, uniting the particulars of the work into a whole. It mediates between the universal (which says everything) and the unique (which cannot be said), establishing a union between repetition and difference (1977: 186).

Thus genre is a "literary code," in relation to which the work of literature is seen as a case of obedience or of change (transformation as option and as alternation) (1977:249, 233). Reading, in contrast to "interpretation" (hermeneutics) and "description" (semiotics), is the determination of "points of focalization" in terms of which the work becomes meaningful. There are many possible readings of a given work, many different points in terms of which it may be organized (239). Reading reflects genre; it is a "de-coding" according to rules which is analogous to the "encoding" which the author performed (249). This confuses the matter somewhat, as it seems to introduce on the one hand the intentionality and consciousness of the reader (as well as that of the author; is genre a set of analogous intentions?) and on the other hand to relativize the structure of genre (since the work can now be read in several different ways). Is this consistent with the idea of genre as the transformation of a universal grammar? How can a single genre permit multiple readings of a given work?

> . . . there is no necessity that a work faithfully incarnate its genre, there is only a probability that it will do so. . . . A work can, for example, manifest more than one category, more than one genre. (22)

[7] Cf. Eliot's essay; also Malraux: 68.

Genre thus appears to be a set of possible frames or structures which may be imposed upon the given work (as "prehermeneutical" and thus not yet an identical entity) in order to establish points of focalization—perhaps by suppressing or deciding the "spots of indeterminacy"* which Ingarden noted?

Although a structuralist, like Todorov, Erhardt Güttegemanns does not say much about genre as such; however, he carries the logical/formal implications within structuralist thought perhaps as far as they can go. He is almost entirely uninterested in pragmatics.

Güttegemanns's theory is called "generative poetics," because his chief interest is in the generation of the poetic text through a series of logical moves or transformations. Genre is for him the specification of "motifs,"* which lie at a deeper structural level than the surface ("expression") level of the text, and beyond which lies the "motifemic"* or deepest level of semantics. Genre therefore again mediates, between the motifemes, or fundamental propositions, and the actual order, the syntagm, of the text (52–53). A genre is a text type within the universe of discourse, a "bundle of [syntagmatic] devices" (7). It defines within the whole the function or action of the sign, which is its significance.

Because the meaning of the text lies in the relation between its surface and structural depth, this meaning is fundamentally thematic or propositional (cf. Scholes, 1974:113). Therefore, following the lead of Wittgenstein, Güttegemanns argues forcefully for the translatability of texts. Non-propositional, indeterminate, "poetic" elements are not considered. Along the same lines, he indicates the possibility of reducing the story to a purely logical form. Utilizing the thirty-one motifemes identified by V. L. Propp in his study of Russian folk-tales, Güttegemanns attempts to relate them logically to one another, using the classical Aristotelian square of opposition. Through a series of complicated (and themselves not entirely logical) maneuvers, he adapts the logical square into a hexagon, in terms of which he is able to explore the possible variations of binary motifemic arrangement; this brings us close to what Todorov describes as theoretical genres. The hexagon is then modified further into a "logical cube," which is applied to actantial* transformations within narrative (72–87). The narrative thus mediates between contradictory and logically contrary motifemes and actants through a dialectic in which they cancel out or balance one another; this mediation is the meaning of the text (cf. Lévi-Strauss: 61). The work of literature is therefore a "productive disjunction" or game (Güttgemanns: 92).

Ambiguity or polysemy has only a provisional value as a narrative strategy, for Güttgemanns. The "point" of the strategy is to win the game, which seems (again) very much like a communication of meaning between author and reader. Nevertheless, he insists that grammar as structure is (methodologically) prior to history (82, 201). He also denies the possibility of a definitive "primal edition" and affirms the possibility of endlessly generating new versions of the text from its logical basis (204–5). This motifemic basis has no historical (or metaphysical) status, according to Güttgemanns.

Certain points may be noted, at which the two circles (of pragmatics and of semantics) approach and even intersect one another. Nonetheless, there also appear to be points at which they diverge, although no two of the theories discussed above can be set against one another as polar opposites. It was noted earlier that the circle of pragmatics faced certain difficulties in dealing with the problems of language, creativity/novelty, and translation/identity. The circle of semantics faces these same problems, but in different ways.

If the first circle's approach to language is nominalistic, then the second one's approach might be called realistic. To be sure, genre remains a convention. However, it is not so much a social-historical convention, as it is the intersection of atemporal logical permutations with contingent situations. The priority of the logical is evident; language is seen as geometrical, spatial, labyrinthine. Even in the case of Frye, myth does not appear to be likely to undergo any change, no matter how many transformations its derivative genres may endure. It is beyond history. Likewise, for Todorov, genre connects an eternal theoretical base with specific historical situations. Jacques Derrida has attacked this structuralist project as a latter-day form of Neoplatonism (1978:27). On the other hand, the circle of pragmatics remains within the historical world. In both circles, however, genre is beyond literature. For the circle of pragmatics, it is teleological; for the circle of semantics, it is logical/thematic. For genre to operate as a principle of sameness, it must presuppose a fundamental otherness.

Where the first circle was more or less undecided or ambiguous in relation to questions of creativity and translation, the second circle provides very clear answers. By starting with a definition of genre as mediating between the universal and the particular, both Todorov and Güttgemanns can respond to the problem of novelty, although it may be that they have thereby ignored one of the horns of Wittgenstein's dilemma: is there never a text in which language is so incarnate, so nearly unique (e.g., poetic language) that a separation of thought and language is impossible, or irrelevant? If the self-referentiality of story lies, as Jakobson indicates, in the poetic function of language (as we noted in the preceding chapter), does this mean that genre theory—to the extent that it can answer these questions—must ignore or seek to overcome referential ambiguity? Yet the structuralists acknowledge the spatiality and polysemy of story. Güttgemanns's exceptional position with regard to translatability seems untenable, although it may deserve more attention than it has received.

3. The Metaphysics of Genre, and the Genre of Metaphysics

What is the metaphysics of these genre theories? The diversity of theories reflects a diversity of metaphysical positions, but underlying this diversity and sustaining it is a common reference to ultimacy, a search for all-encompassing explanation, for a fundamental principle of genre itself, which is metaphysical.

We find the fundamental metaphysical identity of genre in the image of the circle itself. The division into two circles was somewhat arbitrary and for the purpose of summarizing genre theory, and it was noted that this division, although at times clear, at other times tended to become lost or obscured. It was impossible to speak of the pragmatics of genre without eventually turning to a semantic analysis, and every semantic analysis returned to a pragmatics (cf. Gadamer: 235–39). Here we find yet another circle: the impossibility that either of these circles could be adequate in itself to genre, as, following Gödel, we might have predicted. It is this search for self-sufficiency or totalization that characterizes metaphysics, and the difficulty that any single theory of genre has in achieving this totality is regarded as an insufficiency, a lack. Each theory thus generates its own circle, overlapping to some degree the others—perhaps even depending upon the others—but yet different in some important respect from any other theory. This is the genre of genre theory (cf. Derrida, 1980).

The universal factor is the circle. The image of the circles, and of their overlappings, suggests yet another image, that of the sphere. Is not Güttgemanns, as he moves toward the use of a "logical cube," already moving from a two-dimensional to a three-dimensional space of analysis?[8] Whether theory remains within the circle or "advances" to the sphere, it is still drawing upon an image of enclosure, of totality, and therefore, according to Gaston Bachelard's phenomenological study of the poetics of roundness, it is a metaphysics.

There is, according to Bachelard, a dialectics of inside and outside, which seeks to establish "a situation of all situations," a myth of spatiality and alienation (1964:212). Man is a surface of consciousness, and meaning is the enclosing of that surface upon itself—i.e. the sphere. It is the human project that seeks to grasp reality, to contain it, the establishing of a cosmos around a center, the center of being, which is a place of calm repose, and of self-concentration (1964:239; 1969:156–57). It is the round universe of ancient cosmologies, with the phenomenal consciousness of the human at its center; it is the sphere of Parmenides. In modern form, it is the extremes of the total concentration of duration and its material dispersion, between which lies the realm of metaphysics, according to Bergson.[9]

It is this metaphysical roundness which characterizes all of the genre theories noted above. All of these genre theories center around the problem of incorporating the different into the same, and this is expressed in terms of the dialectics of part and whole, of novelty and repetition, of the individual and the categorical. A genre theory is felt to be insufficient if it cannot adequately account for the workings of this dialectic, and if it cannot show how the circle is maintained despite all disruptions. In doing so, genre theory also establishes an inside and an outside, in terms of which the literary work can be identified, in terms of which it gains reality.[10] Without genre there is no understanding, no

[8] Compare Mary Gerhart's image of genre as generating an "optical" cone which "focuses" the text.

[9] Bachelard draws heavily upon Bergson. See Chapter One. Cf. also Bachelard, 1969:205–6, 208.

[10] Cf. Girard: 159, 270. As Derrida says, inscription is a "habitation" in such a case (1976:290). Cf. Bachelard's discussion of the poetics of houses (1964); also Heidegger, 1971a:127–28.

meaning; the words may exist, but without meaning they play no part in the lived world. Genre then consists of a method of locating the literary object within the space of the real world, within an integrated sphere or horizon.

The same theme is developed by Derrida, who states his critique of the onto-theology* of Western thought, the metaphysics of presence, in terms of the metaphor of "differance."* (Derrida's thought, and the possibility that even its thoroughgoing metaphoricity may be inherently metaphysical, will be examined in Chapter Five.) For him, differance is the inversion of genre; whereas genre seeks the identity which underlies all difference, differance asserts a fundamental difference within the heart of identity. Insofar as metaphysics is the denial or forgetting of this differance which constitutes the history of thought, genre must reflect that forgetting by inverting differance. All of the genre theories discussed above can be characterized in this manner.

Both Derrida and Bachelard suggest, although in different ways, that this metaphysics of space and presence also contains within it the principle of its own disruption and/or surpassing. For Derrida, this is the "trace" or "mark," the inscription or residue of writing which cannot be accounted for as presence, which does not "belong" to the genre (1980:212). For Bachelard, it is the claim that the being of man is not a circle or enclosure, but rather a spiral, an asymmetry or "errancy," which would fundamentally disrupt any circle. Human existence, Bachelard implies, lies in a contradiction between concentration and errancy, between the circle and the spiral (1964:214–15). Both Derrida and he hint at a transcending of the metaphysical, indications of which may be found within metaphysics itself. Might it not then be suspected that even within the theories summarized above, there are hints or traces of a non-metaphysical source or mark of genre?

All theories of genre, despite their diverse standpoints, methodologies, etc., assert or seek a unity of meaning either within the text (the circle of semantics) or between author and reader (the circle of pragmatics). If there is a genre theory which does not fit either of these categories, or which lies somewhere between them, it must nonetheless conform to the spatial metaphysics of the hermeneutical circle, with its symbolism of closure and unity. This is a metaphysics of identity and of presence: that of the text to itself (structuralism) or of the author to the reader (phenomenological/historical criticism). Those points at which genre theory becomes obscure or self-contradictory are precisely the points at which the metaphysics of genre is thrown into question and exposed as what it is.

In order to expose this mark of metaphysical identity and to uncover its non-metaphysical trace, we must escape from the circularity of genre. Jean-Paul Sartre and Michel Foucault, often thought of as occupying opposed positions, both suggest how this may be done.

In *Search for a Method*, Sartre in effect poses two ontologies against one another. To be sure, the two—Marxism and existentialism—have a common historical source in Hegelian thought, but they have reacted against the Hegelian system in different ways. Marx sought the objectification of history in the dialectic of material conditions, and Kierkegaard affirmed the irreducibility and irrationality of the individual subject. Sartre brings these two approaches to anthropology (the question of human existence in history) together through what he calls the "Progressive-Regressive Method." This method functions as a dialectic between the universal (Marxist historical categories) and the particular (existential comprehension of uniqueness), and thus it is a sort of hermeneutical circle. It also, according to Sartre, points toward an eventual totalization, a union of perspectives in which the existential "ideology" is absorbed by— even as it corrects it—the Marxist analysis of man (1963:181). Thus an analysis of Sartre's method could be offered which would place it well within metaphysics.

However, his method rejects such a metaphysics. It requires a *praxis*, lived reality or engagement in life and history—in story—in which the universalizing movement of history and the specificity of the individual are united in concrete action. *Praxis* is "distance within immediate proximity" (33, note), the ability of consciousness to surpass the givens of history—states of objectification and alienation—and to pro-ject itself toward a future or in terms of an absence, i.e. toward that which it is not. Thus there is at the heart of *praxis* a negativity. *Praxis* does not thereby escape from history, but rather it mediates, in the life of the individual, between one historical moment and the next (98, note). It is the point at which philosophy "becomes the world," the point of intersection between two objectivities, the biography and the period, which are the two directions involved in the regressive-progressive dialectic, and yet *praxis* is not reducible to them; indeed, it is not an object of knowledge at all, but the subject of what Sartre calls "comprehension" or "non-knowledge" (174). Comprehension rejects the generic.

Man, for Sartre, is a signifying being, and he is continually attempting to signify himself. As the being whose being is in question, man is the only being for whom history is possible (167). History comes from human non-self-identity, from desire or need, which founds every human project and which always seeks totality. That totality, however, is fundamentally man's totality with himself—the anthropological—which is impossible (cf. Detweiler: 84–85). Man's movement toward what Bergson would call durational concentration, or eternity, is continually frustrated by his lack of a center, his "detotalization." Sartre confirms Bachelard's use of the spiral metaphor (Sartre, 1963:106).

In *The Archaeology of Knowledge*, Foucault attempts to outline the methodology which he has used in his studies of the relations between the forms of knowledge in various fields and historical epochs. His desire is to remove the individual subject in its fundamental unknowability—that to which Sartre so emphatically points—from the questions of history and philosophy. He begins by questioning all of the continuities in terms of which history is usually considered—including genre (22). He approaches history not in terms of the "document," but in terms of the "monument," that is, in terms of fields of relations between "discursive formations,"* which do not imply any teleological intentionality, but which establish the historical possibilities of objects of knowledge, means of enunciation, conceptual structures, and strategic choices. These formations are composed of and make possible what Foucault calls "statements." Statements form the materiality of discourse; they are what link it together (100, 115). At a more general and abstract level than discourse is the archive, which defines a system of discursive formations, the threshold, the point at which a discursive formation comes into/passes out of existence, and the *episteme*,* the overall structure of relations between statement, formation, and archive (128, 186, 191). Although Foucault is very careful to distinguish his approach from structuralism, the threefold level of his analysis is reminiscent of it. However, the *episteme* creates a logic; it is not itself logic. Like Todorov, Foucault argues for a plurality of possible meanings for a given phenomenon: any statement may be described in terms of several different formations. Sartre also argues for the "multidimensional," but resolves it into a "multidimensional unity" (111).

Unlike Sartre, Foucault does not seek a totalization of history—not even an impossible one. His goal is to describe the dispersion of knowledge in various ways according to the systems that make that knowledge, and that dispersion, possible; indeed, the knowledge and the dispersion are the same thing. Thus his concern is with what Bergson would call the material extreme of duration. Foucault's interest in "anthropology" is only insofar as man becomes an object of that knowledge/dispersion and is able to occupy historical positions in which that knowing/dispersing becomes possible.

For both Sartre and Foucault, however, there is a refusal of the circle. Neither can rest in the enclosure of presence; in fact, both present powerful critiques of that metaphysics. The fact that they do so in different ways should not be disturbing; it is what should be expected if it is actually possible to escape from the circle. The general discomfort of genre theorists with the idea that a work might legitimately have multiple meanings—especially the case of Todorov, despite his advocacy of polysemy—suggests that there is a relation between metaphysics and singularity of meaning; we noted this relation also in Chapter Two. To the extent that polysemy is possible, we may escape from metaphysics. Metaphysics (and the circle especially) is after all a principle of control, of what might be called "direction"—is not this a major function of genre, as described above? If a non-metaphysical philosophy is possible, homogeneity of thought or commonality of direction should not be expected. Nonetheless, there are some remarkable similarities between the thought of Sartre and Foucault, and between both of them and Derrida, who is also often set over against them. This may, oddly enough, permit a suspicion that none of them has after all escaped entirely from metaphysics.

How then do Sartre and Foucault (as well as Derrida and Bachelard) show the way to a non-metaphysical element or "mark" of genre? What can be found in their thought that indicates a liberation from the security—which is also the imprisonment—of the metaphysics of presence?

This liberation is indicated by violence. It is the radical discontinuity of the discursive formation, the irrational irruption of the statement into history (Foucault); it is the conflict and juxtaposition of the historical epoch and the individual subject, each of which implies and contains the other (Sartre); it is the asymmetry of the eccentric human spiral within the centered roundness of the universe (Bachelard); it is the violence of inscription which lies at the foundation of presence as speech (Derrida). Violence lies at the metaphysical center of genre; what is called for then is an exploration of the violence of genre (cf. Derrida, 1980:213).

If metaphysics is grounded in violence, then the metaphysics of genre is also the violence of genre. Metaphysical identity is produced by a violence which transforms disorderly reality into ordered space-time, which hides non-presence* within the appearance of presence.[11] Genre is the violence which stabilizes and makes significant the noises and marks which become speech and text, language and literature. Therefore a non-metaphysical theory[12] of genre must uncover the non-totality hidden by the violence of genre. The hermeneutical circle must be "sprung" (de-centered), bringing to an end the closure of meaning and making evident the threat of chaos (the end of presence). Meaning is then seen as a distortion or tension masking the permanent impossibility of unity/totality. Genre suppresses within itself an uncontrolled and uncontrollable vibration or oscillation between contradictories, demanding order, an enforced censorship. This idea will be developed further in the next chapter.

As noted above, hints of this may be found in the genre theories discussed above. Some theories do a "better job" than others of hiding the violence of genre and suppressing the chaos beneath meaning. For example, Todorov explicitly notes the violence of theory in applying general categories to individual units, which can be arguably categorized in different ways (1973:22). This difficulty is precisely what is reflected elsewhere

---

[11] Cf. de Man, 1978:22, Bergson: 28ff.

[12] We must be cautious about calling this a "theory," as *theoria* itself carries overtones of presence and passivity (Gadamer: 111). We are not at a point, however, where a more appropriate term can replace it. We will continue to use this term, remembering that violence is also being done to this word.

in his genre theory, when he encounters the problem of reconciling polysemy with the notion of genre as a "code," which was noted above. Wittgenstein's uncertainty about translation also reflects a sense of violence. The entire semi-discontinuous format of the *Philosophical Investigations*, with its suggestive but inconclusive segments, implies a recognition of the non-totality of the real.

In contrast, the theories of Güttgemanns and Gadamer, despite their evident differences, are overwhelmingly comprehensive and consistent. The element of disruption, the ragged edge of violence, is nowhere visible. That they argue forcefully for the complete communicability and/or translatability of meaning suggests a thorough suppression of the violence of speech and writing, which is reflected in the corresponding violence of genre (of reading).

In between these extremes, the theories of Hirsch and Frye, which are again quite different, occupy moderate positions. The ambiguity of "metaphorical assimilation" of the new variation into the established genre, and the insistence upon objective validity, but of a "willed type"—a horizon of meaning, not a specific content—may indicate points of uncertainty in Hirsch's thought. The incoherence of Frye's general theory, caused at least in part by an indecisiveness on the methodological relationship between structure and history, may also indicate fissures within his metaphysics. Hernadi claims that Frye's "polycentricity" is an asset, not a drawback (153). Perhaps at these points the violence of genre is uncomfortably present.

Of what would a theory of genre as violence consist? In the discussion earlier in this chapter, a number of fundamental characteristics of genre theory—problems that any theory of genre might be expected to solve—were noted. These included the fundamental alternations between pragmatics and semantics (the nature of meaning), between history and logic (nominalism vs. realism), and the need to integrate the same and the different (tradition and creativity). Can a theory of genre as violence adequately account for and answer these problems?

The nature of meaning, in such a theory, is seen as a hierarchy of conflicts. The basic conflict is the alternation between pragmatics and semantics, between the existential demand for completeness and consistency and the "spots of indeterminacy" which inhabit (or infest) the story. Meaning arises from the conflict between the act of communication and the structure of a given ("natural") language. The structure requires (through the "law" of genre) that the act, to be meaningful, conform to certain patterns (schemata); the act, in its uniqueness, distorts the structure to suit its purposes (intentionality). Genre "determines" the story (cf. Chatman: 94–95). In this dialectic is given the general form of genre as violence. Within pragmatics, there is the further tension between author and reader (i.e. the "real," not the implied, author and reader). The first position is seeking to communicate something to the second—to bring the second position into conformity with itself. The second, in contrast, is seeking to understand the first—to integrate the communication into its own contextual frames. Each seeks to do violence to the other, as Sartre notes (150ff.). Within semantics, there is a similar violence (also of conformity vs. distortion) between the possibilities established in the structures of language itself and the uniqueness of the individual sequence of words. This violence emerges in actual objective communication (the story as "implied dialogue") which necessarily stands between and thereby determines the two subjective positions constituting the pragmatics; yet those subjective poles, as consciousnesses (beholders), form the language into writing/reading (speech/hearing) as intentional acts, and the sequence is conformed to the universal structure. Each conflict alienates and mediates the other one. This alienation/mediation is the essential nature of violence.[13]

The same dialectic of violence is apparent in the tension between history and logic as the sources of meaning. The text emerges at a definable historical point, before which a genealogy can be traced. It may also come to an historical end in various ways, which we described in Chapter One as its passage, as garbage, beyond the metaphysical realm. It belongs to a tradition, which, however, it must surpass in order to come into existence. This is the tension between present and past, between novelty and tradition, which establishes an opening for the creation of a future. Central to this historical tension is the conflict between the class and the instance, the generic and the unique, the center and the "eccentric"—a logical tension. Again, there is a violence within logic, and a violence within history, and a deeper violence

---

[13] Cf. Girard: *passim*.

between logic and history. Each seeks to contain and reduce the other.

Finally, the same pattern—the identity or genre of genre— emerges also within the problem of the same and the different. Indeed, these three characteristic questions seem to slip into one another in a theory of genre as violence. Identity is a distortion of difference; to argue that two texts are the same is to do violence to both. Translation, insofar as it attempts to maintain a sameness across different languages (or in the case of paraphrase, different language-games), is essentially violent. Even to argue that a given text is the same at two different points in time (or for two different readers) is to commit the violence of history (or logic). Derrida notes that a fundamental difference renders impossible self-identity within the "simple" act of language itself. On the other hand, sameness constitutes difference; without identity, difference is impossible. Simply to say, "This is different," is not possible without supposing an underlying possibility of sameness, posited by the copula. Yet the logical identity signified by the copula is undercut and disrupted by the fictionality/metaphoricity of language, as we noted in Chapter Three. "The same" seeks to destroy the possibility of "the other," and vice versa. This is the double movement of genre which Todorov notes (1973:7).

Genre as violence mediates between the abstract possibility of language (*langue*) and the concrete actuality of word sequences (*parole*). Even to say this is to say too much, however, for neither the language nor the word sequence can be conceived or understood except in generic terms, as Todorov has noted. Only the generic can be said, because only the genre unites the concrete specificity and abstract universality in meaning. It is a "form of judgment" (Derrida, 1973:91–92) or belief, in which the ideal or *a priori* is brought to the real or empirical (or vice versa) in various ways.[14] This union is what may be called the text or story. Meaning cannot be separated from story since it is already present in the act of selection which frames

---

[14] Genre (and belief) make communication possible, yet are themselves very difficult to speak about, for precisely that reason; they require a sort of meta-genre* or meta-belief which is necessarily different from the original and must appear heretical, blasphemous, irrational, unscientific, etc. See Søren Kierkegaard's meditation on the inability of Abraham to explain himself, in *Fear and Trembling*; also Derrida, 1976:87; Heidegger, 1971a:81; Todorov, 1977:87.

the story as such. This we have called the establishment of a canon. Therefore, generic differences seem "natural" and "obvious"; the violence which constitutes the genre is invisible. Genre is implicit in the text; not in the "words themselves" or in the linguistic possibility, but in the selection which realizes the possibility in story.[15] Genres are the different ways of violence through which meaning is established in and as story, the different ways in which story can be "real." Corresponding to these ways of violence would be points of resistance, which point toward the ultimately non-generic language and meaningless words, the chaotic non-world from which world (and self) are constructed in story.

4. Violence and Belief

But this is still to speak of genre as an aspect of literary theory. Can a theory of genre as violence extend beyond the realm of literature, to other realms of experience? Both Frye and Hernadi point tentatively in this direction. Although the present chapter has avoided detailed study of generic typology, perhaps a suggestion towards a generic theory of reality would help to answer this question. I do not wish to discount other traditional (literary) genres, and I cannot claim that referentiality is the only (or even the primary) determinant of genre; however, I do claim that referentiality is an essential determinant of genre, and that it must become prominent when metaphysical entities (persons, theories, institutions, etc.) "migrate" from one genre to another.

If genre is violence, then genres are acts of violence committed against reality, or conceptual "lies." Genres inevitably conceal while revealing. It is these deceptions which modulate generically, in terms of what is concealed and revealed, the tension between the real beholder and the implied dialogue of the story, as a function of what Wayne Booth calls "distance" (155ff.). Wittgenstein speaks in passing of the lie as a language-game, with its own set of rules; here, however, it might be more appropriate to speak of a family of games, played within what Hugh Kenner has called the "closed field" of language (Scholes/Kellogg: 158–59).[16] Following

---

15 Cf. Ingarden: 154–55; Malraux:335–39.
16 Cf. Crossan, 1975:13ff.; Rorty: 345.

the lead, then, of Nietzsche, Sartre, and others, we might posit three great reality-genres (which would of course have to be subdivided into lesser genres).[17]

The first genre would be the genre of deceit, or the conscious, deliberate pretense that reality is other than it is. This is the category most commonly called the lie, but its extension is broader than is normally conceived. It is the attempt of one party to lead other parties to a misperception of the world; therefore it implies, among other things, that the first party has a notion or theory of "how things really are," which is then disguised. In this genre, the fundamental fictionality of language and story is most completely hidden beneath layers of more apparent deception—that of the narrator.

The second genre would be close to what Sartre called "bad faith"—to fail to recognize that one's conception of "how things really are" is itself a distortion and act of violence, to think that one's understanding accurately reflects objective reality. It would be to have the illusion of the possibility of honesty (nondeception), both in relation to oneself and to others. This genre is dominated by the practical and the effective, by means and ends, by causes and results. It is the realm of intentionality, of freedom, and of expectation; it is the realm of the complete object. Both myth and science—despite their tendencies toward, respectively, the ideal and the real, as noted in the previous chapter—belong to this genre, which is characterized by what Ingarden calls seriousness; it "forgets" its own violence in the division of story into "real" facts and "real" fictions. Beneath its self-conscious duplicity, the first genre presupposes the second one.

A third genre would be related to "good faith" (Sartre, 1956:69–70), the recognition of the story as story, the admittance that one's conception of reality is a lie, and the recognition of the necessity of the lie. In order to live, we must fabricate for ourselves a world, even if it cannot be given with objective certainty. We therefore must lie to ourselves, but at least we can admit that we are doing so. This is the closest approximation to an impossible truth-within-lie, and it is no doubt a genre with very few instances. Instances would consist of those stories in which self-referentiality—spatial form, the breakdown of

---

[17] Cf. Husserl: 275 (Sec. 104).

the genre of "good faith" forces a retreat into narrativity & founds narrative theology.

frames—would be most evident, and thus it would be, paradoxically, an anti-generic genre—the frustration of genre. As we have noted previously, works of this self-referential genre establish an ambiguity within, or may totally break down, the metaphysical frames of the distinction and connection between context and content; it is opposed to univocity, linear temporality, and monotheism. As a result, further distinctions relevant to the genres of reality within this genre are impossible.

"Literature" as traditionally conceived belongs to the second and third genres—the forgetting, and the non-forgetting, of fictionality. These genres cut across traditional literary genres altogether. They are quite obviously ethical categories, as perhaps should be expected from a theory of violence. Metaphysics is contained within the first and second genres—as is traditional theology—and therefore the conventional distinction between fact and fiction—belief—belongs to the second genre, as was argued above (cf. Sartre, n.d.:90–91, 149). Both the first and third genres subvert belief, but in different ways: the first in the name of a contrary belief, the third much more radically. To put it another way, belief—which here appears also as sincerity or honesty—stands in between (mediates) the lie (as commonly understood) and the fiction.

Fiction and non-fiction (facts and lies) exist alongside one another, as different genres or sub-genres of a deeper fictionality. Because we are concerned here especially with the question of belief, and the connection between fiction and fact, this typology belongs especially to the circle of pragmatics; fiction and fact are generically distinguished in a circle of expectation and fulfillment (or disappointment), a metaphysical circle which is identity, reality (cf. Scholes/Kellogg: 257). Within the circle of pragmatics, genre is primarily a function of the relation between sense and reference. Although the circle of semantics is clearly also a generic operation, as a function of the relation between sign and sense, it operates at a "deeper" (pre-generic?) level, which we will consider further in the next chapter. In any case, the division of genres presented above is offered as a tentative suggestion only, and much more valuable typologies might be possible.

If a non-metaphysical theory of genre as violence is possible, then a generic analysis of (phenomenal) reality and the overcoming of the common distinction between fact and fiction is permitted. Such a theory permits the extension of the concept of story beyond the conventional bounds of literature to any aspect of human experience. This theory at the same time regulates the possibility of that extension. Genre is after all fundamentally a law[18] which controls the interplay of the universal and the particular, and as such it establishes limits for the ways in which story may be extended, and within which intersubjective communication is possible. A typology of genre as violence will have to be a typology of the ways of violence. Even lying is a game, and therefore it has rules.

To speak of genre as violence may be unpleasant, but it appears to be necessary if the metaphysical dimensions of genre are to be made clear. However, does this approach in fact free us from metaphysics? As the mediator of the same and the different, genre is fundamentally metaphorical. The hermeneutical circle, in all of its variations, is a metaphor, and a spatial metaphor at that, transforming the temporal acts of reading and writing into a cyclicality (cf. Vernon: 18). "Violence" as used here is also a metaphor—physical violence is not supposed, although no clear distinction can be made between the violence of genre and, e.g., censorship or the punishment of blasphemers, etc.—but the violence of genre is nonetheless a real violence. Does this suggestion of the reality of violence not also raise the possibility of a metaphysics hidden here: hidden perhaps within the metaphoricity of violence? Does meta-phor also "carry" meta-physics, inevitably? In penetrating the metaphysics of presence, of roundness (of inside and outside), by turning to the metaphor of violence, have we simply opted for a more subtle metaphysics and even less detectable presuppositions about the concept of story?

---

[18] Derrida argues that this law is itself madness (1980:228). But is madness a sort of language-game, with its own rules, or is it the limit-condition, beyond the borders established by all rules? Note Foucault's discussion of madness, in *Madness and Civilization*, and Derrida's discussion of Foucault's discussion, in *Writing and Difference* (to which Foucault has since replied). Also see Aichele, *Theology as Comedy*, chap. 7.

Chapter Five
THE METAPHOR OF STORY

What is the relation, or connection, between metaphysics (and the genre-violence which it requires) and metaphor*? Can metaphor, or the metaphorical sequence that is story, provide an "escape" from the scholastic enclosure of metaphysics—that is, can it move us "beyond metaphysics," can it answer fundamental questions about reality without producing even more fundamental problems? Perhaps establishing the "closure of metaphysics" would create a clearing within (or about) modern thought, an intellectual, metaphorical space in which thought could be freed from its ancient bondage to metaphysics. Or is metaphor in the last analysis metaphysical, and does it hide metaphysics from us with an intellectual sleight-of-hand? Is metaphysics somehow "built into" us—does being human include a longing for identity and presence that must haunt us?—and are a philosophy which seeks to escape metaphysics and any thought structure built upon that philosophy condemned in advance to a merely critical role?

1. Metaphor and Metaphysics

Jacques Derrida sets metaphor against metaphysics in his examination of the closure of metaphysics and the fundamental "differance"* (*différance*) which generates metaphysics and therefore limits it. He wants to go beyond metaphysics, in the sense of breaking through these arbitrary limits and escaping differance by exploring it. Derrida's writings constitute a network of metaphors interlinked with one another. Each of these metaphors places a challenge or threat before metaphysics: the primacy of writing over speech and the endless repetition (or dissemination*) of the text, the essential violence of meaning as reading/writing, and the differance or supplementarity which dislocates the signifier from any possible signified.

"Differance" both means and exemplifies a difference (of the written letter) which is not a difference (no change in sound), a fracturing of identity that does not destroy it. Differance implies that writing—contrary to the usual assumption—is logically and ontologically prior to speech, that there is a textuality (or texture) of experience which is inscribed (or punctured) in violence and which is always being read—i.e. it is always incomplete; it is never "present." Presence, for Derrida, is the metaphysics of modern thought, hidden in the "logocentrism"* which stresses the fundamentality, the originality of speech.

The metaphysics of presence implies spatial and temporal unity. Identity/presence is established in space and time as a relation with and denial of death (1973:35, 54). I am present to this object, here. I am self-present to myself, now. Presence "orders all objectivity of the object and all relations of knowledge" (1976:57). Derrida's description of the metaphysics of presence resembles Bachelard's discussion of metaphysics as enclosure or intimacy. Metaphysics is concentration: a unitary center which establishes a circumference, which separates an inside from an outside. To demonstrate its closure, and in opposition to this metaphysics, Derrida insists that presence itself emerges from and is generated by differance. Space is the product of difference, the difference of distinctions between objects and between contexts. This difference permits the possibility of language and the communication of meaning: syntagmatic and paradigmatic difference. Temporality is the product of deferral, the separation of past from future which creates memory and duration. For the present to be present (e.g., my present), it must engage in the other (the non-present*) as the past in repetition or as the future in anticipation. The present cannot be present without being not present (1973:60ff.; cf. 1976:66; Bergson, 1949:55–56). Non-presence lies at the heart of presence. Differance, then, is the play of difference and deferral.

Differance belongs, in Vernon's terminology (see Chapter Two), to the space of the map and its logical extreme, the labyrinth. It is a "mergence"* which rejects and radically undercuts the Heideggerian spatio-temporality of Vernon's "garden." Derrida speaks of the book as a labyrinth, an arrangement of ciphers in which we seek to trace a primal text, which is itself, of course, a representation, a non-identity (1973:85, 104; 1978:298). The tracing is both an act of creation and a passive following. We are reminded of the image of the labyrinth as it recurs in the self-referential* stories of Jorge Luis Borges. To describe differance is to describe the source and spring of (phenomenological) space and time; yet how can this be done in language which is itself the product of differance and therefore thoroughly "inhabited" by space and time? To move beyond presence, we need a language that is not a language of presence. The parallel to the mystics' "negative way" is a strong one, and Derrida is aware of it. Differance is "unnamable" (1973:133–34, 159; 1976:14).[1] Like the mystics, he uses metaphors and puns.[2]

The comparison to mysticism is not made lightly; the koan and the riddle are not far from Derrida's style. If by theology we mean the attempt to think systematically about the objects or occasions of faith—our "ultimate concern"—then theology and mysticism have always been in tension. The mystic, in attempting to speak the ineffable, the experience of the Godhead, must utilize negative language: God is "not this . . . not that." The attempt to posit something through a language of negativity inevitably undercuts itself, resulting in a metaphysical stutter or hesitation which is very frustrating to the systematic thinker. This hesitation, this silence, points beyond metaphysics.[3] Is Derrida pushing this negative language as far as it will go; is he a mystic?

The mystic longs for the presence of the divine; theology

---

[1] One is reminded of Samuel Beckett's novel, *The Unnamable*, which also is "about" a relentless search to speak that which cannot be spoken—non-identity, "what I am," the Sartrean *pour-soi*. Cf. Foucault, 1979:141ff; Todorov, 1977:189.

[2] ". . . the play upon words makes us think somehow of a negligence on the part of language, which, for the time being, seems to have forgotten its real function [of reference] and now claims to accommodate things to itself instead of accommodating itself to things. And so the play upon words always betrays a momentary *lapse of attention* in language . . ." (Bergson, 1900:139, emphasis Bergson's).

[3] Mysticism is a threat to theology; yet it continually informs theology. We see this in the work of numerous contemporary thinkers, such as Martin Buber, who speaks of God as the Eternal Thou (the "thou" can be neither manipulated nor conceptualized), and Paul Tillich, whose terminology for God oscillates between images of "ground" and of "abyss." Even the most systematic of theologies are high metaphorical, as the Medieval theologians recognized with the notion of the *analogia entis*. Doctrines which are central to the Judeo-Christian tradition, such as creation *ex nihilo* or the two natures of Christ, repel any systematic formulation, as does the problem of evil.

seems to require the absence of God, an absence which presupposes the metaphysics of presence. Derrida's analysis of metaphysics, however, is a questioning of presence. Speech, or what Husserl calls "expression," the ideality of speech, is presence, according to Derrida. In speech, there is complete unity between the ideal signifier and the signified, between intention and meaning. Husserl's view is similar to that of Artaud, who seeks a reunification of force and meaning in "flesh" in his call for a "theater of cruelty" (Derrida, 1978:179). For Husserl, writing and other external forms of communication are "indication," secondary and inferior to expression; for Artaud, the text or the "work" introduces a duality—it steals my self from me by separating force and meaning. For both Husserl and Artaud, presence is prior to the non-presence (as distinguished from absence) of writing.

The Platonic Myth of Theuth (from the *Phaedrus*), in its attack upon the *pharmakon*—which is both "remedy" and "poison"—of writing, conceals a metaphor of writing which, according to Derrida, is woven throughout the entire Platonic textual corpus. By writing, Plato gives homage to his dead "father"—Socrates, the speaker, who drank the poison—and leaves (or "sows") his attack upon writing without a living "presence" to rescue it from the misconstructions of the ignorant. Writing is a labyrinthine "pharmacy" of mirrors, an abyss of representation, in which presence is irremediably lost in repetition. The text as mirror is also a veil or membrane, a hymen which separates even as it is penetrated (in writing, in reading), the infinite displacement of the (absolute) signified and thus of the (metaphysical) enclosure, Plato's Cave. It is always a spatial "scene." Writing consists in a fundamental undecidability, an original non-identity and impropriety, which is the letter (the mark) that inevitably supplements and resists the present idea, and the presence of the idea; it is this play of the letter, differance, which undercuts metaphorically the metaphysics of identity and the semantics of reference.

The traditional theory of metaphor—that the metaphor is a supplementary meaning, a surplus* or transference added on to the "proper" meaning of a word—also makes this assumption (1976:15). Following Heidegger, Derrida refers to this as the onto-theological* system of philosophy—the necessity of Being. All that is real stands within a metaphysical enclosure of original identity, to which language properly points with referential univocity. According to Derrida, only when we are able to question this system and explore its effects on thought can the closure of metaphysics be completed and therefore deconstructed.* In order to do this, we must avoid making the same assumptions: hence, differance, the excess* within meaning, the fundamental metaphoricity of all writing.

Writing is representation: an image, a repetition, a fiction. Derrida rejects any notion of a primal presentation. *Everything* is represented; there is no original, no fundamental truth.[4] Writing is the essential detour of speech (*logos*, the reason). It is in this detour, or rupture, this metaphoricity, that metaphysics is grounded (1973:136; 1976:9; 1978:166). Writing established a rupture within reality, a separation between the letter and the concept that allows and demands meaning. What there is—what the history of philosophy is—is a series of traces, and of traces of traces, a fabric/weaving/ textile, the text produced by differance. To uncover the traces of differance within metaphysics, or presence, is to deconstruct philosophy.

Writing is non-presence; it is pre-hermeneutical and meaningless.[5] Reading, in contrast, involves both presence and absence; it is post-hermeneutical, meaningful, metaphysical. The movement of deconstruction is opposite to that of "hermeneutics," as thinkers such as Gadamer and Hirsch have defined it.[6] Much of Derrida's writings consist of his frequently unorthodox but always careful readings—"neither simple commentary nor simple interpretation" (1973: 88)—of the writings of others. These readings are acts of violence, translations or re-presentations which violate and shatter the ideal whole, the text as a "volume."[7] Deconstruction is "solicitation," the shaking of a theoretical system in order to unfold its structure and phenomenological genesis. The violence of reading necessarily corresponds to the violence of writing; Derrida speaks of "inscription" as though it were an act of cutting into a surface or plowing the ground. Hence his recurring image of the

4 "'Genesis and Structure' and Phenomenology" (1978).
5 Cf. Derrida's discussion of the *étron*, or turd, in *Spurs*. Also see Deleuze: 279–82.
6 This is why Ricoeur attacks Derrida. Rorty confuses this matter with his indiscriminate use of "hermeneutics." See the second part of this chapter.
7 See the two essays on the poetry of Edmond Jabès in *Writing and Difference*. Also 1981:149–50.

spur or the point: the point of the pen spearing the paper, which bisociates into the "point" of the story and the present as a "point" in space-time. Meaning and presence emerge from and always conceal (or "efface") the violence of inscription.[8] Yet the spur is also the trace, or residue (1979:39–41); the oscillation of metaphor between inscription and weaving is confusing, and important. The meaningful reading contains yet overlooks the meaningless writing.

Derrida's is a critical philosophy, but not a systematic one. Its creativity is in its reading of others. The discovery and following of traces may not be a sufficient end of thought, but to go beyond it may be to "fall back" into metaphysics.

> Now here, precisely, is announced—as promise or threat—an apocalypse without apocalypse, . . . of addresses without message and without destination, without sender or decidable addressee, without last judgment. . . . Here the catastrophe would perhaps be *of* the apocalypse itself, its *pli* [fold] and its end, a closure without end, an end without end. (1982:94–95, emphasis Derrida's)

Derridean deconstruction evidently "goes nowhere." It circles round and round within the closure of logocentrism, noting all the faults and creases, the blanks and folds, and steadfastly refusing to attempt an escape. In his essays and books, Derrida repeats himself endlessly, monotonously. That is precisely his point: there is no new, no original discourse, no first, non-textual presence, only an endless reading and re-reading, eternally recurring and regenerating itself, disseminating itself innumerably, intertextually. Deconstruction is a *praxis*, an immense labor. This is the end without end: to mark the limits, yet never to arrive. If we take Derrida seriously, how could we do otherwise? The exceeding of the limits of the metaphysics of presence is not to be accomplished by any discourse, any *logos* (not even that of the father/king/God), but only in the unutterable, unnamable remainder/resistance (*restance*) of letters, numbers, which are empty, asemic.*

To interpret Derrida systematically is to misunderstand; when one enters the elusive, elliptical realm of differance, one

---

[8] Cf. Girard's discussions of the essentially mythic misunderstanding of the original sacrificial crisis.

must not expect to come to a "point," a resting-place.[9] This does not mean that interpretation is impossible; only the interpretation or reading which seeks to possess the truth, to achieve univocity, is. According to Derrida, woman is for Nietzsche the representation of deconstructionist hermeneutics. The "essence of woman" is dissimulation, distance, play (*epochē**), and the affirmation of undecidability and the plurality of truth. Nietzsche uses the image of woman to advocate style instead of meaning, the inaccessibility of ultimate meaning, the impossibility of totality. In his meditations on woman, the Jews, and related subjects, Nietzsche was rejecting a proper philosophy (a philosophy of property, of presence—e.g., Heidegger) and calling for a philosophy of indefinite openness and parody and of separation, in which that which is meaningless or rejected (the physical word on paper, which we ignore and surpass in the search for its meaning) is recognized in its differance.

Derrida discusses this further in his commentary on the "deconstructive" novels of Philippe Sollers, and especially upon *Numbers*, in which traditional literary conventions are replaced by a numerical arrangement determined by the number 4. Plot, characters, author, and theme disappear into "arithmological" patterns. In this opening or emptying of the text into numbers, the principle of repetition, is revealed the dissemination of writing, beyond either univocity or polysemy, the shattering of the metaphysical, onto-theological frames of story.

> The concept of polysemy thus belongs within the confines of explanation, within the explication or enumeration, in the present, of meaning. It belongs to the attending discourse. Its style is that of the representative surface. It forgets that its horizon is framed. . . . To the extent that meaning presents itself, gathers itself together, says itself, and is able to stand there, it erases difference and casts it aside. . . . The seminal [writing], on the contrary, disseminates itself without ever having *been* itself and without coming back to itself. Its very engagement in division, its involvement in its own multiplication, which is always carried out at a loss and unto death, is what constitutes it as such in its living proliferation. It exists in number. (1981:351, emphasis Derrida's)

The broken frame of elliptical writing—the undecidable

---

9 "Ellipsis" (1978). Also 1973:128.

oscillation of identity and difference—opens on to an "absolute outside" (357), a further text which traces and erases the other, and so on to infinity. This is Frege's divergent infinite series.* Thus there is an end without end, which "is constitutive of my 'unity,' my 'unit-ness,' that is, my inscription and my substitution within the series of numbers," and "of possibility and of impossibility for any transcendental subjectivity" (364). Reading is always an "inter-text"; outside of the text there is nothing— except another text.

2. The Elimination of Undecidability

Differance, then, is a series of traces or texts endlessly repeating and yet detouring, disruption within disruption, an excess or sacrifice[10] that constitutes the very texture of the text, the "volume" of metaphysics. We have already seen that "writing," for Derrida, consists of a perpetual undecidability between metaphors of plowing and weaving (phallus and hymen, pen and paper). "Differance" or the "supplement" likewise oscillates between images of presence, or identity, and absence, or difference, with spatio-temporal implications. It is not one or the other, but both as they simultaneously undercut one another.[11] Through this fundamental structure (if we may call it that) of undecidable symmetry or logical oscillation—this infinite divergent series—this exchange or economy of representation, Derrida seeks to shatter (to solicit) metaphysics. Each of the opposing metaphors seeks to subordinate the other, creating what René Girard has called—in another context, but not irrelevant to this one[12]—a crisis of reciprocal violence, which can

[10] As Bataille uses that term; see "From Restricted to General Economy: an Hegelianism without Reserve" (1978).

[11] We have also noted the oscillation which Derrida uncovers within the Platonic pharmakon. Also cf. 1976:292; Bachelard, 1969:47, 60; Deleuze: 286–90.

[12] Girard develops the concepts of reciprocal and sacrificial violence in a study of the history of culture, with special reference to Greek mythology and tragedy, as well as African, South American, and other folk tales, and "primitive" myths. He clearly distinguishes between the "real" (actual or potential) violence occurring in historical cultural groupings and the "mythic" (or metaphoric) violence which is a culturally necessary substitution, so that humankind may safely misunderstand the truth about human violence (5–6). Thus he remains within the sphere of the conventional theory of metaphor, and within metaphysics. However, he admits that truth may be found in myth (233). Compare Derrida, 1976:36, to Girard: 47–49, 79–81.

only end, unless otherwise stopped, in their mutual destruction. According to Girard, this crisis can only be stopped or prevented by an act of sacrifice, an arbitrary selection, an elimination, which establishes a principle of order, a structuring of reality, expressed in a myth. The myth-frame sacrifices the original, undecidable chaos to an order—which is, as Kafka has also noted (33), a misunderstanding. This order could also be expressed as a circle which contains and excludes, and which is the essence of metaphysics. Thus metaphysics is essentially metaphorical, but a metaphysical system—an onto-theology—requires a construction of metaphors within which metaphorical oscillation is impossible and which is deconstructed whenever such oscillation occurs. This would necessarily be true of any story in which the oscillation is "decided"—sacrificed—and therefore eliminated. When metaphorical oscillation occurs, the metaphysical "outside" seeks to contain the "inside," and vice versa; the system undercuts itself in an infinite regression of metaphors and metaphors of metaphors (counter-metaphors), etc. Differance is therefore unnamable and certainly unspeakable, like the name of God.[13] "What exceeds the closure is *nothing*: neither the presence of being, nor meaning, neither history nor philosophy; but another thing which has no name . . ." (1976:286, emphasis Derrida's).

The reality beyond or behind metaphysics, then, is not what Heidegger calls Being, but non-presence or the non-metaphysics of writing revealed in deconstruction as the infinite regress of metaphoric oscillation (1976:314). It is the dispersed materiality of writing, which we earlier called the hyletic* phase of the sign, and which is continually and unavoidably eliminated, erased, forgotten, even as it traces the systems of onto-theology. Metaphysics can only proceed from a deciding, the refusal of undecidability, the sacrifice of metaphoric oscillation. This occurs within what was described in the preceding chapter as the second genre of belief, the genre of "bad faith," in which the frame sacrifices the oscillation within the "complex reference" of belief (Frege) and establishes the priority of meaning as reference. That such a metaphysical decision is unavoidable is implied by several commentators upon Derrida.

---

[13] Crossan claims that Yahweh is beyond metaphor (1976:56), Girard identifies this "non-difference" with the sacred (245).

Robert Detweiler notes that Derrida comes as close as anyone to a position which unites structuralism and phenomenology. If he does, it is by establishing an oscillation between the text's intended essence (its self-identity) and its relation to an other (its absence from itself), or between what Frege called "sense" and "reference." This oscillation between content and context is the self-referentiality of the text, the differance of its textuality. Detweiler tends, however, to agree with Paul Ricoeur that reference must have priority over sense. He criticizes Derrida as a "holistic structuralist" (167) and praises Ricoeur's "elementaristic" position.[14] Detweiler concludes his own list of methodological steps for integrating structuralist and phenomenological approaches to literature by insisting on a choice which "transforms the desire for the object into a message. The interpretive act concludes as a confession of how reality shall be joined" (207). Oscillation must be brought to a stop.

This is also the crux of Ricoeur's criticisms of Derrida. In his apology for discourse, Ricoeur adopts a largely Husserlian theory of expression, claiming that Derrida has missed "the grounding of both [speech and writing] . . . in the dialectical constitution of discourse" (1976:26). Writing "interferes" with the semantics of discourse by producing a self-referential literature, in which the original situation of discourse may be lost.

Ricoeur agrees with Derrida on the fundamental metaphoricity of language and the metaphysics which arises in metaphor (1977:138, 287), but his theory of metaphor is based on the traditional theories which Derrida attacks (1976:15). Although he substantially modifies this tradition, Ricoeur must still presuppose the necessity of a "literal" or "primary" meaning, the dominance of which is destroyed by the metaphoric contradiction of interpretations, which in turn requires a "work of meaning" through which the metaphoric text is able to disclose a world to the reader (1976:87–94). "The metaphorical interpretation presupposes a literal interpretation which self-destructs in a significant contradiction" (1976:50). In establishing an origin and a meaning (a series of dependent meanings), Ricoeur remains within the metaphysics of presence, even if the origin is irretrievably lost in writing. The "insistent metaphor" reveals the

---

[14] Detweiler borrows these terms from Willis Overton.

depths of existence; discourse is primordially rooted in life. Metaphor is characterized not by excess—Derrida's term suggesting a fundamental non-identity—but by a surplus of meaning.

Richard Rorty and Carl Raschke adopt strikingly similar approaches to Derrida. The philosopher Rorty makes only slight reference to Derrida, identifying his ideas with the "hermeneutic" philosophy of the later Heidegger, Wittgenstein, and others, which he contrasts favorably to the normal, "epistemological" philosophy that has dominated the history of modern philosophy as the "mirror of nature."[15] Hermeneutics, in Rorty's view, opposes the metaphor of conversation (an infinity of vocabularies) to the epistemological metaphor of inquiry (universal commensuration). Hermeneutics seeks edification, not system, and as an "edifying philosopher," Derrida decries "the very notion of having a view, while avoiding having a view about having views" (371).

The theologian Raschke uses Derrida extensively in an attack on structuralism and the reduction of language to signification.

> The sign abolishes its own intent of signification—what it *represents* is "nothing" at all. . . . No metalanguage appears to invest what we can say or write with certainty or truth. (27, 29, emphasis Raschke's)

However, Raschke seeks to pass "through" Derrida in order to arrive somewhere else: to arrive at Heidegger, the Heidegger who affirms language as the presentation or "mean-ing" of Being. Derrida refuses to admit the possibility—or at least the presentability—of Being (which is, Raschke insists, not a metaphysical entity, but the "e-vent" or process which makes language possible); therefore, Derrida is a "nihilist" (45, 86). Raschke concludes by announcing "the end of theology" as "dialogy," in language very close to Rorty's discussion of the metaphor of conversation; deconstruction serves as the iconoclasm necessary if dialogic language is to reveal Being.[16]

Thus Raschke can call for a "reconstruction"* of theology (although it may no longer be called "theology"), the dialectical creation (á la Heidegger) of a new being or reality, a Nietzschean breakthrough made possible by the "gravedigging"

---

[15] Cf. Crossan's brief discussion of this distinction (1975:35–37; 1976:166).

[16] Raschke reiterates this position in Altizer et al.; see also the essays by Scharlemann and Myers in that collection. Cf. Crossan, 1976:47.

(in Altizer, et al.:30) of the deconstruction of traditional meta-physics (and theology). Thomas Altizer uses different language to make similar claims:

> That absolute necessity or *causa sui* which is the classical Christian identity of God has now passed into the center of the world, and that passage has brought the world to an end, or brought an end to every identity which stands forth only as itself. Such an ending is a fully apocalyptic *parousia* or total presence, . . . the death of God, the eschatological end of the God who is God. . . . And that is an apocalyptic and eschatological end, a final and total end, and therefore an end which can only be named by the Christian as the realization of absolute grace. (174–75)

This move toward reconstruction, however, is a return to what Derrida might call eschato-teleo-theology, a re-enclosure of logo-centrism, a submission to the metaphysics—and Derrida insists that dialectics is also metaphysical—of presence. The radical subversiveness within deconstruction is foreclosed by these theologians in the name of metaphysical reconstruction.

An alternative theological strategy is also possible. Charles Winquist announces a "third-order theology," which will be a "hermeneutics of texts" rather than the traditional (metaphysical) attempts to mirror or imaginatively to construct a reality. This will be a hermeneutics of expansion and of suspicion, which will pull theological constructions "back toward the economics of force," towards their "metaphorical roots" in the text and its materiality (Altizer et al.:55). John Leavey has adopted a similar approach to the problem, and something along these lines will be pursued somewhat further in Chapter Six. For these theologians, deconstruction is not penultimate ("Deconstruction is as important a movement as reconstruction."—Winquist, in Altizer et al.:47), but rather it is the end, or as Derrida says, the end of the end, the end without end.

The strengths and weaknesses of these approaches, and Derrida's own metaphoric strategy, are made apparent in the writings of the New Testament scholar, John Dominic Crossan. In his search for a "philosophical and theological option" to interpret the "special linguistic or semiotic aspects" of the para-bles (1979:101), Crossan contrasts Derrida to Ricoeur on the question of whether metaphor represents an absence or presence of meaning: it is Derrida's understanding of writing as absence which accounts for the paradox and inexhaustible plurality of meaning which are characteristic of parable, according to Crossan. He sees Derrida leading theologians to a "contemporary retrieval of negative theology," which is "a theology articulating itself by a philosophy of absence" (1980:10).[17] Even the oral genre of parable is better explained in terms of a phenomenologically prior textuality. Derrida's concern with the play of language and the incompleteness of metaphor[18] further supports Crossan's argument that parable is essentially polysemic (1976: 124–27; 1980:23).

Yet, as we have seen, for Derrida, even polysemy remains within the closure of logocentrism. Writing, furthermore, is not characterized by absence, but by non-presence. "Absence" remains within a dialectical metaphysics of presence; writing is not absence, even as it is not presence.[19] It is true that the metaphor of play operates throughout Derrida's writings, and that Derrida suggests at points that play is what Crossan calls a "mega-metaphor,"* a single metaphor controlling all the others, and all possible meaning (1979:44; 1980:66). If this were true, we would return to the domain of metaphysics, for such a metaphor would short-circuit the symmetrical oscillation of metaphors and establish in its place a hierarchy. Indeed, it is the idea that story as a self-limited surface or enclosure is peculiarly able to create a world which governs Crossan's approach to the parables; parables are those points of self-referentiality (the stories of story) which enable us to become aware of the story as such, and of that which transcends story (1975:46–47, 122; 1979:7–8, 94). Parable establishes a contradiction between the "expression" of the text and the reader/hearer's "expectation."

That Crossan remains within metaphysics is apparent in his

---

[17] Cf. Crossan, 1979:109. Crossan notes that Derrida rejects the possibility of theological implications to his thought. He cites, as an example of such a negative theology, the work of Louis Marin.

[18] Crossan also notes the similarity between Derrida's understanding of metaphor and the Incompleteness Theorems of Kurt Gödel (see Chapter One). Derrida also mentions Gödel (1981:219).

[19] Cf. Sartre's discussion of this in *Being and Nothingness*: "absence" supposes that I expect a "presence." Therefore absence can occur only within a hermeneutical engagement, in contrast to non-presence, which makes no such presupposition.

insistence on identifying the origin of the parables with the "historical Jesus"—despite the claims of Derrida, Foucault, and others that history itself is the product of an *episteme*,* of differance, and despite his own discussion of Borges's treatment of history as a metaphor[20]—and in his attempt to find a "fundamental morality" in the parables—for which he turns to Heidegger (1979:113). He remains within metaphysics because he overlooks in Derrida's writings the metaphor which Derrida sets into oscillation with play (and which likewise appears at many points in his writings), the metaphor of death. Play is the absence of presence; death is the presence of absence. Both death and play are metaphors of finitude, of an inside and an outside.[21] Death does appear in Crossan's writings within an existentialist context (1975, 1976) and more recently as the chaos which limits art as the self-consciousness of play (1980:85–87). Here, however, he establishes a metaphysical, logical opposition between inside and outside (presence and absence, sense and reference) rather than the non-metaphysical oscillation of two symmetrical metaphors, each an image/variation of the other, each seeking to claim the other. The play of death must be undercut by the death of play, and vice versa, with no resolution. Instead, Crossan subordinates death to play (1976:22–23).[22]

Thus Crossan, like the others discussed above, has difficulty with the metaphoric oscillations at the center of Derrida's deconstructions, and he tends to reduce them to or replace them with a single, dominating metaphor. Crossan regains much of this loss by

[20] Crossan is evidently aware of this sort of criticism; cf. 1974:192–93. His response at this point, however, does not seem consistent with his repeated insistence upon the "historical Jesus." Why is one level of the tradition preferable to others? What are the metaphysical implications of that preference?

[21] Perhaps the clearest statement of this duality appears in Derrida's discussions of the "two interpretations of interpretation" where, however, he tends to treat "play" as the non-metaphysical. Nonetheless, he claims that the two interpretations are not to be chosen between. See note 7. Crossan discusses these passages in 1980:63–64.

[22] Could we develop a new generic typology of stories dominated by mega-metaphors of play and death, respectively? Or is this what the classical authors meant by comedy and tragedy? And is tragicomedy (see K. Guthke, *Modern Tragicomedy*) or what I have called "dark comedy" (*Theology as Comedy*) the point at which the two mega-metaphors attack and undercut one another? Crossan's position at the end of *Raid on the Articulate* seems very close to this view (181–82).

seeking an oscillation within metaphor itself—not as Ricoeur does, in a conflict of interpretations which requires a creative expansion of the horizon* of one's world—but in the paradoxical convolutions of the metaphor within itself (1979:49ff.).[23] However, to use a single metaphor to undercut and question itself, as Crossan does in his studies of the parables of the Sower (the interpretation of interpretation) and of the Treasure (the abandonment of abandonment) does not permit an escape from metaphysics; for although one may convolute the metaphor upon itself endlessly—as Crossan would—one remains within the limits of its metaphysical closure. The play of play is still (self-identically) play. Non-presence is captured within presence; differance is identified with difference.[24] The infinite regress which Crossan seeks within metaphor must be found between metaphors.

It appears that it is within a structure of undecidable oscillation between symmetrical metaphors that the deconstruction of, and any escape from, metaphysics—a metaphorical construction and enclosure—is possible. To turn to a single metaphor, or mega-metaphor, as Crossan and others noted above have done, is insufficient, for even if one discovers an infinite regress within the metaphor, the undecidability has been lost. Yet "oscillation" is also a metaphor. With what then must oscillation itself oscillate? If we follow this line of questioning, then Crossan and the others appear to be right in seeking a mega-metaphor: the oscillation of oscillation. Or is there also an undecidable differance between/within two metaphors of oscillation?

Derrida cites Husserl's reference to the art gallery, in which there is a painting of an art gallery, in which there is a painting of an art gallery, etc. (see Chapter One). The metaphors of gallery and painting—context and content, reference and sense—infinitely regress upon one another. Crossan compares metaphor to the room of mirrors in the Schönbrunn Palace in Vienna; one sees nothing but the reflections of reflections, parallel, infinite regressions within content and context. This coincides with Foucault's discussion of the Velázquez painting (see Chapter One) in which a

---

[23] Via's approach to parable is not terribly different from Crossan's at this point (Via, 1967:24–25, 75–87). However, Via's structuralism "binds" his approach to parables much more narrowly—less playfully—than does Crossan's, and he adopts the conventional theory of metaphor, as modified along lines similar to the approach of Ricoeur.

[24] Cf. Derrida's discussion of Heidegger's "fundamental metaphor" (1976:22).

mirror plays a crucial role, and also with Rorty's image of philosophy as the "mirror of nature"; to turn the mirror upon itself is to
invite conversation (or in Raschke's term, dialogy). In Heideggerian terminology, language reveals Being as the being of language.
However, as Derrida notes, to say, "There is only the mirror"—i.e.,
language—is doxic,* and therefore metaphysical. If we can set
these two metaphors of metaphor—Crossan's and Derrida's mega-
metaphors—against one another, if we can "inscribe" differance
between them, then they can "supplement" one another. Oscillation then undercuts the metaphysics of oscillation itself; we set
metaphysics against itself, as Derrida does, and we set metaphysics
against the non-metaphysics of differance. Only if differance so
self-destructs can it "remain" differance.

3. Deconstruction and Myth

The deconstruction of metaphysics requires the uncovering
of the undecidable metaphoric oscillation which lies hidden
within it. To the extent that any story is self-identical and meaningful—that it has a sense and a reference—it is a metaphysical
entity. Myth, through its reconciliation of binary opposites, creates a world of space and time and therefore the possibility of all
other meaningful stories; it is the story of stories and the ground
of metaphysical reality.

It is parable, according to Crossan, which subverts the
spatio-temporal world established by and in myth (1974:211;
1975:59–60). Therefore, parable deconstructs myth; it is "dis-
edifying." Crossan's descriptions of parable as transformation
of/within myth—as anti-myth—and as itself the binary opposite
of myth—as a distinct genre—themselves oscillate; thus parable,
in his analysis, does not stand as a genre, but as the exposing of
the generic oscillation within myth itself. It is this which we
noted earlier as the paradoxical self-referentiality, the hidden
fictionality, of all stories, in the undecidable oscillation of context
and content, of sense and reference.

If this is the case, then parable (as paradoxical discourse)
cannot lie "outside" of myth or metaphysics, as a separate genre
or realm, but it must lie (also) "within" it, as a sacrificed, exces-
sive, supplementary metaphoric oscillation. It is the labyrinth of
juxtaposed, disconnected, and conflicting spaces within the "garden" of myth, the fused whole which the reader produces

(Frank, 1963:25). We must find within the myth an oscillation—an oscillation of oscillations, an "opalescence,"* in Ingarden's words—which may be parabolically, paradoxically uncovered in the infinite, asemic dissemination of writing, the materiality of the sign.

In Chapter Two, we began to explore one such myth, the story of the Garden of Eden, in terms of the question of spatial and temporal form. We drew upon a paradoxical commentary on the myth by Franz Kafka.[25] Numerous scholars have noted the importance of the Eden myth to Kafka, as a focal point for his concern with law, guilt, and the absurdity of human existence.

Kafka's commentary has no plot or characters of its own; indeed, it cannot claim to exist in its own right, but only as a supplement, "another text," a fragmented, paradoxical questioning. However, unlike other commentaries on the Genesis story, it makes no pretext of completeness; it does not, as Derrida says, "belong to the attending discourse," casting non-metaphysical difference aside. Rather, it is entirely incomplete; it makes evident the fundamental differance within the myth.

> The expulsion from Paradise is in its main significance eternal: Consequently, the expulsion from Paradise is final, and life in this world irrevocable, but the eternal nature of the occurrence (or, temporally expressed, the eternal recapitulation of the occurrence) makes it nevertheless possible that not only could we live continuously in Paradise, but that we are continuously there in actual fact, no matter whether we know it here or not. (29)

The paradox of the Eden story is the paradox of time and eternity, or as we said in Chapter Two, the origin of time in space, of the garden in the map. It is necessary that we be temporally and irrevocably removed from the Garden in order that we may be in it eternally. The irony is that we may not know that we are in it, although it was because of knowledge that we were cast out. Because we were expelled, Paradise could remain intact (beyond time). Because it remains eternally intact, we temporal beings are condemned to frustration.

[25] These fragmentary comments on the Eden story appear under the title "Paradise," in the collection of short Kafka pieces, *Parables and Paradoxes.* "Paradise" is translated by Willa and Edwin Muir, as is "On Parables," from the same collection, quoted below. The epigram for this book, "The Building of the Temple," was translated by Clement Greenberg.

> . . . nobody can remain content with the mere knowl-
> edge of good and evil in itself, but must endeavor as
> well to act in accordance with it. The strength to do so,
> however, is not likewise given him, consequently he
> must destroy himself trying to do so, at the risk of not
> achieving the necessary strength even then; yet there
> remains nothing for him but this final attempt. . . . An
> attempt to falsify the actuality of knowledge, to regard
> knowledge as a goal still to be reached. (31–33)

In other words, we forget the "knowledge" which we already
and always had, the Tree which, since we ate of it, is now (eternally) "in" us.

The paradox of time and eternity leads to and is reflected in
the paradox of within and without, a revision of Zeno's paradoxes
of space. "We are sinful not merely because we have eaten of the
Tree of Knowledge, but also because we have not yet eaten of the
Tree of Life" (29). The Trees divided the center of the Garden; yet
we have eternally eaten of the one and the other is forever beyond
our grasp. We are simultaneously at the center and (indescribably)
distant from it (Greenberg: 167–68). As a result, Kafka says, man
did not die (as the serpent promised) and yet he did (as God promised); we did not become God-like (eternal life), and yet we did
(divine knowledge). Man is doubly chained: one chain ties us to
earth, and the other to heaven. "So that if he heads, say, for the
earth, his heavenly collar throttles him, and if he heads for
Heaven, his earthly one does the same" (31).

The two paradoxes stand in a curious relationship to each
other. They are the same and yet not the same; each leads into
and yet inverts the other. They oscillate. They correspond to two
metaphoric sequences: (1) to the extent that the Tree is in me (I
am God-like, eternal), I am out of the Garden (I am cursed,
temporal), and to the extent that I am in the Garden, the Tree is
not in me; and (2) the Tree is in me, and I am not in the Garden, yet the Tree is in the Garden. Thus I am in the Garden and
not in the Garden, and the Tree is in me and not in me.

David Jobling has noted that structurally, the Tree of
Knowledge is outside of the Garden, since the man knows that to
eat of it is to "die" (44, 47). Thus an oscillation is set up within
the sense of the story, between the plot* and the fable,* which is
resolved (sacrificed) when the dichotomy good/evil is established

and secured by the cursing of the humans and the serpent. What Kafka does is to reject this non-logical sacrifice and expose the hidden oscillation(s). He says:

> When the sage says: 'Go over,' he does not mean that we should cross to some actual place, which we could do anyhow if the labor were worth it; he means some fabulous yonder, something unknown to us, something too that he cannot designate more precisely, and therefore cannot help us here in the very least. (11)

Is this Nietzschean "Go over" any other than "Come," the reverberations of which in the Book of Revelation, and in all apocalyptic, are noted by Derrida (1982)? (Cf. Crossan, 1974:213.) Paradise comes eternally; yet it does not come temporally. We go over in eternity, but not in time. Yet time and eternity are not different, but differant. Is this not "an apocalypse without apocalypse . . . an end without end"?

Greenberg notes that for Kafka there are no books in Paradise, no rupture between literature and life, between knowledge and truth (50; cf. Emrich: 39–40).[26] Thus there could not be two separate, different Trees, and there could be no Fall, no loss of Paradise. Kafka's world is unfinished, pre-mythical (Benjamin: 117). According to Glatzer, writing is for Kafka "a form of prayer," arising from the unbridgeable distance between man's knowledge and the Tree of Life (53). The Trees are differance "itself," the fundamental supplementarity or labyrinth deconstructing the Garden. There are no books, no self-enclosed volumes, and yet the Trees "are" writing, the labyrinth at the center of the Garden.[27]

Another paradoxical unfolding of the Eden myth appears in Jesus' parable of the Treasure: "The kingdom of heaven is like

[26] Compare to Borges, for whom the letter, the book, and the library are associated with God (see Chapter One). Bachelard also speaks of Paradise as a library (1969:25). Cf. Derrida, 1981:281.

[27] Glatzer argues that for Kafka the Tree of Life—the truth of "creative passivity"—is hidden within the Tree of Knowledge—the truth of activity (57–58). "The first truth [of activity] we acquired in reality, the second is ours only by intuition." However, "the first truth refers to a moment of time, the second to eternity; thus the first truth vanishes in the light of the second." This would appear to overcome the paradox, resolving into a theological interpretation of Kafka as mystic. Strauss adopts a similar thesis: Kafka's writing "was only a rehearsal of the silence in which his spirit might find the repose that it strove for" (206; cf. also 214–15, 220–21). On Kafka as "schizophrenic," see Vernon: 126ff.

treasure hidden in a field, which a man found and covered up; then in his joy he goes and sells all that he has and buys that field" (Matt 12:44, RSV; cf. Gospel of Thomas 109).[28] Crossan presents a detailed discussion of this parable in *Finding Is the First Act*, comparing it not only to Jewish precedents, but also to the larger sub-genre of treasure-trove stories, and to the adjoining parable of the Pearl (Matt 13:45–46; cf. Gospel of Thomas 76), with which it may or may not form a "double parable."[29]

Crossan argues that the trove story structure consists of six motifemic* units—hiding, seeking, finding, obtaining, securing, using—and their opposites, not all of which need to be present in a given story (1979:17). These units may be sequenced in either a plausible (e.g., hiding/seeking) or a paradoxical (not hiding/seeking) order. It is the paradoxical sequences which are of most interest (cf. Via, 1967:105). The sequence of a particular story is "chosen" from all of the possible variations on the "canonical [motifemic] sequence," the deep structure of the genre. This choice reflects a value, which can be placed in a hierarchy between the superficial value of "contest," through "luck/providence" and "superstition," and the deepest value of "paradox" (Crossan, 1979:44–47), in which reality is destroyed.[30] The paradox of parable thus belongs to the third, anti-generic genre described in Chapter Four (120). If myth is the fundamental misunderstanding arising from the sacrifice/framing of metaphoric oscillation, the parabolic paradox is the revelation of the misunderstanding, and of its inevitability.

In these terms, the Treasure parable begins with the paradoxical sequence of hiding/not seeking/finding.[31] The motifeme of obtaining is complicated by sub-motifemes of non-ownership,

---

[28] I do not claim that Jesus "intended" this parable as a commentary on the Eden myth, nor do I attempt to reconstruct the "original" parable. Because of the inevitable metaphysical violence of translation, the Revised Standard Version account of the story may or may not be the "same" as in other translations or the Greek, and the implications of my discussion of it will be accordingly limited.

[29] Jeremias is not sure (90); Crossan denies this (1979:102–5). Bultmann calls them "formally parallel" similitudes (194). Whether the Treasure story is properly a parable in the narrow sense is not relevant here.

[30] Crossan draws here upon the typology of play developed by Roger Caillois (49–50).

[31] The sequence is, strictly speaking, a double paradox, for it implies the absent possibility of not hiding/seeking/not finding (Crossan, 1979:31–33).

rehiding the treasure, and selling all, in which moral (and possibly legal) issues are involved; yet these issues are ignored in the parable. Thus the parable moves from the value of superstition (buried treasure) to that of contest (selling so that one may buy), and in comparing the kingdom of heaven to the treasure (or the finding of one), it suggests that we abandon for it not only our goods, but our morals and even more.

> Finally, most enigmatically, vertiginously, and therefore least clearly, comes a third and outermost circle of challenge which threatens the very *parable* which contains it. The Kingdom demands our "all," demands the abandonment not only of our *goods* and of our *morals* but, finally, of our *parables* as well. The ultimate, most difficult and most paradoxical demand of the Kingdom is for the abandonment of abandonment itself. (93; Crossan's emphases)

This doubled abandonment is not the rejection of abandonment, but an infinite regress within the metaphor of abandonment, a radical *praxis* of the Jewish tradition of "aniconicity" within language itself. It is the unending failure of story, its fundamental non-metaphysics. It establishes what Crossan calls a "negative dialectic"

> with and against a tradition which is both continually generated by it and also continually regenerated through being undermined by it. (109)[32]

The Treasure parable is thus a "metaparable" of parable itself, negating the very genre to which it belongs and revealing the power of parable to negate any genre. Its very failure is its success, as Kafka says: to win in reality is to lose in parable.

How may Derrida's analysis of metaphor supplement Crossan's, as applied to this story, and how, in terms of that, does the story appear as a paradoxical commentary on the Eden myth, like Kafka's?

Several decades ago, John Wisdom and the participants in the "University Debate" (Flew and MacIntyre: 96ff.) created the parable, or allegory, of the "invisible gardener," as part of the

---

32 Crossan explicitly follows Stanley Fish's use of "dialectic" for "a language that, by calling attention to the insufficiency of its own procedures, calls into question the sufficiency of the minds it unsettles" (119, quoting *Self-Consuming Artifacts*: 378). Kafka also had such a notion, according to Emrich (62).

then-current discussion of verifiability in religious language. The
story contains two characters, who come across a "clearing in the
jungle" which contains "many flowers and many weeds," and
they begin to argue whether or not it is a garden. Depending
upon the perspective adopted, the same state of affairs supports
two contradictory claims: (1) it is a (never-tended) vacant lot, or
(2) it is a (secretly-tended) garden.

Could we not raise a similar question about the field in
which the treasure is found?[33] It is, to be sure, *ho agros*, a field,
not *to paradeison* as in the Septuagint version of the Eden myth.
It is also not virgin wilderness, for a treasure is hidden there.
Why does the finder rehide the treasure and buy the field, unless
it is already owned and the owner has rights to its contents? It is
this question, as Crossan notes, that suggests the finder's amoral-
ity, or immorality. It is for this reason that the finder must abandon all.

If the field is not understood as the garden, then Crossan's
profound analysis of the Treasure parable stands intact. However, if the field both is and is not the garden—the Edenic
Garden—there is an oscillation between the content and the
context of the story which supplements the infinite regress of
abandonment. We are then caught in Kafka's paradox of time
and eternity. "The man" eternally remains "in" the Garden even
as he happens to pass through the spatio-temporal enclosure of
this particular field. The much-noted resistance of parable to
symbolic, allegorical, and/or exemplary interpretations[34] is evident here: the specific, concrete world of the story does not simply "stand for" an abstact, ideal, and/or eternal realm. The two
interpretations of the field (vacant lot, garden) exclude one
another even as they endlessly displace one another, requiring a
sacrifice if understanding is to be achieved. Neither interpretation can "complete" the parable and remove the indeterminacy,
for each establishes an infinite regression of metaphor.

---

[33] Cf. Via, 1967:58–61. What is the relation between the Treasure parable and
Mt. 19:21? The young man is told to "sell all you possess and give to the
poor"—to abandon all—"and you will have treasure in heaven." Cf. also Lk.
12:33, Mt. 6:20. If these passages are juxtaposed, the field is Paradise.

[34] Crossan, 1974:87–88; Via, 1967:2–16, 106; Bultmann: 198; Dibelius: 254–58.
For similar comments regarding Kafka's writings, see Emrich: 79ff.; Greenberg:
13–15; Strauss: 207. Greenberg and Strauss note the similarity of (Kafka's) parables to dreams.

We have already seen how the "vacant lot" interpretation leads, for Crossan, to the abandonment of abandonment, reflecting his image of metaphor as the mirror room in the palace, which was described in Chapter One as a parallel regression within content and context. Where does the "garden" interpretation lead us?

If the field is a garden—the long-lost Garden—then the parable recounts the radical reversal of the origin of space-time. "The man" (like Adam) is originally situated in the field, but (unlike Adam) he does not recognize what it is; he has, as Kafka notes, suppressed or "forgotten" the knowledge which is eternally in him and for which he was originally cast out of the Garden. Adam, with and through knowledge, moved from the (original) inside to the outside; the man, in and through ignorance, moves from (eschatological: "the kingdom of heaven") outside to inside. When he finds the treasure, his ignorance is interrupted and he is "reminded" of where he is.

This reminding is not, however, the Bergsonian memory— the time-generating unity of duration emerging from a concentration of presence (cf. Bachelard, 1969:115)—but rather, it is the Socratic notion of "recollection"—an external, materially-triggered supplementation.[35] The supplement is the treasure, which might just as well be a bag of coins or an ancient, holy relic, but which could also be a chest filled with gems—i.e., a jewel-case,* which would return us to the Derridean "scene of writing."

> E-numeration, like de-nomination, makes and unmakes, joins and dismembers, in one and the same blow, both number and name, de-limiting them with borders that ceaselessly accost the borderless, the supernumerary, the surname. That is the way the (jewel-)case opens and shuts. (Derrida, 1981:364)

[35] In *The Symposium*: "For what is implied in the word 'recollection,' but the departure of knowledge, which is ever being forgotten and is renewed and preserved by recollection, appearing to be the same although in reality new, according to that law of succession by which all mortal things are preserved, not by absolute sameness of existence, but by substitution, the old worn-out mortality leaving another new and similar one behind—unlike the immortal in this, which is always the same and not another?" Socrates "recollects" Diotima's speech to him; do we have here another ironic passage, not unlike Plato writing about Socrates's attack on writing in the *Phaedrus*? On a similar notion of Kafka's, see Emrich: 46.

The "jewel-case" is only one (non-identical) juncture in Derrida's expanding and oscillating network of metaphors for writing—hymen, weaving, point, spur, trace, supplement—all of which suggest images that are at once profoundly sexual and theological. The finding and rehiding of the treasure, so that one may "go and sell all" in order to "buy that field"—especially if the field is the Garden in which one originated and its "owner" is God (the father)—have immense Oedipal overtones. As Girard notes, one averts such a crisis—the doubling of the field and the Garden, the treasure and the Trees—through sacrifice, in this case the "spiritualizing" of the parable as an allegory or example story.

We must not, however, think of the psychosexual and of the theological as two different sets of metaphoric tenors to be borne by the one vehicle of the treasure. Just as Derrida notes the non-identity of the jewel-case, so we must also note the non-difference of the sexual and the theological within the Oedipal myth (as well as the Eden myth). Any "spiritualizing" which would separate the two would require a sacrifice.[36]

The Oedipal act is also a crime—not unlike the crime involved in the Treasure parable—and the man repeats Adam in deceiving the owner/God of the field/Garden. In the Eden myth the deception attempt fails, reinforcing the power of God and leading to the curses, the casting-out of the humans. In the parable, although we have no reason to expect the deception to fail, the outcome is not narrated. Is this a kerygmatic call for decision, and if so, would anyone decide otherwise than to support the man's actions, even though their morality is very questionable? If, as Jeremias suggests (101), the kingdom is not being compared with the treasure, but with the finding/rehiding/selling/buying, the moral issue is unavoidable.[37]

The parable ends with the man neither in nor out of the field (again, compare Kafka's paradox). The value of the treasure,

---

[36] Benjamin states, "There are two ways to miss the point of Kafka's works. One is to interpret them naturally, the other is the supernatural interpretation. Both the psychoanalytic and the theological interpretations equally miss the essential points" (127). Yet both are required, and each requires the other.

[37] "Immorality . . . attaches to the very nature of the representer (performer). . . . Luxury, fine clothes, and dissipation are not signifiers incidentally coming about here and there, they are the crimes of the signifier or representer itself" (Derrida, 1976:304).

which is in the field, is measured as that for which one sells all—
"all" meaning everything outside of the field. The selling and
buying establish an economy or exchange between inside and
outside; however, it is an exchange between the finite (within
the boundaries) and the indefinite (and possibly infinite: "all")—
"borders that ceaselessly accost the borderless." We are again at
Crossan's mega-metaphor of the abandonment of abandonment;
no matter how much the man has to sell, the treasure exceeds it
all. Thus the treasure is a jewel-box, an infinite displacement of
value, which enfolds and is enfolded in "all" of the man's
property. The abandonment of (moral and economic) propriety
and the (eschatological) propriety of abandonment:[38] here we
have the infinite regression of context and content, metaphor as
undecidable oscillation, as suggested by Derrida.

Yet as we noted at the end of the second part of this chapter, these two mega-metaphors do not oppose one another, but
they also oscillate infinitely, regressively, undecidably: an oscillation of non-identical oscillations. Each supplements the other,
but incompletely and endlessly.

Both Kafka's commentary and the Treasure parable center
(and de-center) upon what Derrida calls "writing," the fundamental non-originality of representation, the supplementarity or
differance of the material (hyletic) phase of the sign, the dissemination of letters. Both find this writing at the center of the Eden
myth—the two Trees between which we are eternally suspended, the treasure which is neither (yet both) inside or (and)
outside—and both uncover and explore this non-identity (this
"hymen") at the center and origin of all metaphysical identity.
The Trees and the treasure are, in Derrida's terms, "marks" or
"traces" of the non-metaphysical. They cannot ever be compre-
hended as such by the interpreter—they are fundamentally
incomprehensible—but they must always be surpassed in the
direction of meaning and presence. The logic of paradox de-
centers and breaks the frame, the enclosure of metaphysical
"roundness." It uncovers a deflection or deviation of logic itself,
which gives to parabolic stores their peculiar "paranoid" quality,
their resistance to coherent meaning,[39] and the necessity of a

---

[38] Cf. Crossan on the "fundamental morality" of the parable. His use of Heidegger at this point, however, suggests a return to the metaphysics of presence.

[39] Benjamin says of the "little man" of Kafka's stories that he "is at home in

continual, and endless, re-reading of them. Interpretation is paralyzed, precisely at the point where metaphysics is exceeded.[40] The story's self-referentiality consists in a double, symmetrical oscillation, an irony which cuts twice, destroying the metaphysical integrity of context and content. We never "finish" reading; the story is endless, an end without end (cf. Bachelard, 1969:75). If Kafka's account makes this somewhat clearer than Jesus' does, it is perhaps because of the Christian tendency, noted by Crossan, to turn Jesus into the Parable and thereby to displace and sacrifice his parables.[41] We are more ready to forget the paradox of his stories than in Kafka's case, for highly metaphysical/theological reasons.

Both stories reveal the paradox at the center of myth and therefore of all story. Both belong to that anti-generic genre, that self-referential fictionality noted in previous chapters. In both, the non-identity and non-presence of the materiality of the sign, and the inevitable, violent metaphysics (in decision and sacrifice) of story, are made evident in a crisis of oscillating, regressive, and undecidable metaphor. This undecidability or non-presence of metaphor—of "writing"—endlessly undercuts and exceeds the binary logic of identity, the dialectic of presence and absence, unless it is sacrificed to (framed with a) metaphysical decision.

---

distorted life; he will disappear with the coming of the Messiah, of whom a great rabbi once said that he did not wish to change the world by force, but would only make a slight adjustment in it" (134).

[40] We are also (and likewise) paralyzed when we consider Zeno's paradoxes and discover the (logical) impossibility of movement.

[41] It is at this point—the redaction and later interpretation of the parables—that the need for a historical approach to the parables is evident, as Crossan, Jeremias, and others have noted. We might also note the need for historical study of translation. Cf. Jeremias: 23–27.

Chapter Six
EXCEEDING THE LIMITS

1. The Resurrection of the Word

To conclude—to enclose, to sum up the disseminated*—
would be to unsay what has been said, or to essay what cannot
be said. So much (perhaps all) onto-theo-logizing* is also a logo-
onto-theizing, a divinizing, and therefore a sacrificing of the
word. The alternatives to metaphysics appear to be the silence of
the mystics and the endless chatter of deconstruction,* the
unending oscillation of metaphors,* which are perhaps the same
thing: the attempt to "find" the story and to "say oneself" and
therefore the world. Perhaps the silent mystic has indeed been
able to bring it to an end; the "deconstructionist" cannot accept
such a retreat and yet has no other hope.

Must then either deconstruction be tamed or theology, with
its metaphysical urge to conclude, be destroyed? Deconstruction
requires that the "Absolute Signified" (truth, value, God) must
be, not removed, not denied, but infinitely displaced: non-
present,* neither present nor absent. The Derridean supplement
subverts any logic or dialectic of identity, whether positive or
negative. This displacement of the signified requires the infinite
displacement of any absolute signifier—i.e., of any canonical
scripture. Yet deconstruction cannot leave writing, and it cannot
leave it alone; it circles about and reveals the letter, the meaningless mark, which is forgotten by, even as it creates, the
logocentric* metaphysics of Western thought.

In order to confront this non-identity within metaphysics,
Derrida sets into play a network of infinitely and mutually
regressive metaphors, which deconstruct the onto-theology of
presence. If theology would confront and survive such a deconstruction, it must find within its search for identity—re God,
man, history, etc.—a paradoxical and non-identical supplement
or differance.* Only in this way could the metaphysical limits of

story be exceeded.* This is in fact the direction in which some contemporary theologians have been pointing, as was noted in Chapter Five; they sought not an ultimate reconstruction* of theology—a conclusion—but a new negative theology, requiring the recognition of the non-resolvable, infinitely regressive meta-phoricity of all thought and language, including (and especially) theology.[1]

In the recognition that words can slip out of our grasp, that they can evade our control and refuse our meanings, we discover the senselessness (or asemy*) of the word. We are always trying to grasp it, to get it into our control, but the word is always out of our control. It is always able to destroy our illusion of sense, to break the bonds of our juxtapositions, to fill life with insecurity and chaos. The word is resurrected whenever we sacrifice it to meaning. Of course, once it emerges from the tomb of the old meaning, we immediately reclothe it—"re-incarnate" it—in a new meaning. This is, however, a threat to the meanings through which we construct our selves and our world, and it requires of us that we be always seeking to tighten further our hold on the word, that we ensure our meanings, which are also defenses against the senseless word. Meaning allows us simultaneously to possess the word and to forget it, to ignore its (non-)presence.

If the word is senseless, then it is unimportant; importance is meaning. If all words were unimportant, there would be no difference between them—no difference that would mean anything. Words in their senselessness are equally indifferent to mankind: the Word and the word, the holy and the profane, the blasphemous and the decent, all are one. The Bible and the shopping list, the great philosophical or scientific statement and the scrawlings of little children, the poem and the post-card, all have the same value—that is, no value. They are all garbage. There is no reason to choose one over another; we exclude them all.

In choosing one word and abandoning another, I give them an arrangement, an order, a relevance that constitutes for me an identity (the meaning of my life). We choose words and give them meaning in order to define ourselves. Human life is defined by (and may be defined as) the yearning after and grasping of meaning. The meaning contains a structure—it is a

---

[1] Derrida has denied the possibility of such a negative theology (1982:61).

structure—which is the structure of the world and of the self. This meaning is not something added to an incomplete reality, but it is the way the fragments of reality are put together or juxtaposed. Meaning is not a gap to be filled but a picture puzzle that comes out different each time, and which, each time it does so, changes the reality of the fragments themselves. I choose because I must choose, because it is impossible for me not to live in a world; I choose in order to construct a world in which to live and a self to do the living. In giving the word meaning, we bring ourselves into existence. In the beginning was the word, and through the word all things were created.

Yet the word is never without meaning. We can never fully uncover or encounter its senselessness; it can never be beheld as such. Indeed, the word is polysemic; it is constantly enveloped or "incarnated" in many meanings. Even to assert that the word has no meaning is to give it a meaning of sorts, by placing it outside of (yet in relation to) the meaningful world. Even this is an exclusion, a sacrifice. To incarnate the word in meaning is to place it within the world, to give it a content and a context, a sense and a reference. It is to juxtapose the word with all the other elements that compose the world, to place it in a story. Meaning constitutes the word as a world. Senseless, hyletic* "reality" is then transformed into a meaningful world; the dispersion of its materiality, its resistance to meaning, is violently transcended and united into a whole. This subjects the word to vulnerability, ignorance, and corruption, as well as hope, understanding, and beauty, as these are characteristics of the finite, human world. The meaningful word is in the world and is therefore subject to its limitations.

The word is crucified in meaning; the sacrifice gives it meaning. It is an imperfect word because it is our word. As the givers of its meaning, we gain possession of the word; we control the word. We need to control and possess it precisely in order to find meaning, to make the word meaningful. We use the word to create meaning by telling stories with words; yet the words are not the stories, and vice versa.

The word is therefore subjected to and dominated by the human will to meaning, the hermeneutic circle and the hermeneutic sacrifice. Nonetheless, the word resists this subjection and rejects our juxtapositions and eliminations; this is its resurrection, its infinity, exceeding all limits. For the critic, who is by definition very much concerned with the word, this produces a very serious and difficult tension. It is the paralyzing tension between the word in it hyletic senselessness and the meanings only in which it can exist for us as humans, between the pre-hermeneutical sign and the post-hermeneutical story. The temptation is to ignore the senselessness and the act of choice, to accept the defense mechanisms without question, and to focus one's critical efforts entirely on the meanings. The meanings are, after all, the gods—the Absolute (or Transcendental) Signified—because it is by means of them that the world is created. (They are the formal and final causes, while the hyletic sign is the material cause.) Meaning is man's ultimate concern, the ground of my self's being. In contrast, the asemic word is a mystery, an abyss, the unthinkable. Nothing can be said about it that does not immediately become meaningful— that which it is not. The senseless word is ineffable and unreadable.

Yet the critic, if he or she is to be thorough in his or her work, must maintain this tension between the senseless word and its meaning-incarnations. It is the ability to maintain this tension that makes one a theologian—of the sort being called for[2]—as well as a critic. This theologian-critic must exercise what don Juan, the hero of Carlos Castaneda's adventures in Amerindian wisdom, calls "controlled folly," the involvement of the will in a reality known to be indifferent.[3] It is the controlled folly of the theologian-critic to choose even though he or she knows full well that his or her choice makes no difference, or rather that it creates the difference that it will make. Choice creates a world in which choice makes a difference.

Yet if this world were sufficient to our needs, and if it were logically coherent, there would be no place for this critic. In the knowledge of insufficiency and of incoherence—which is always a knowledge from "within" the story, a negative knowledge— lies the recognition of the limits of story. Parable lies at the heart of myth, and it cannot exist apart from a mythic structure; this is Crossan's "negative dialectic."

To attempt to exceed these limits in a new story—a "better" story, or a mega-story comprising all stories (a super-myth)—will not work, for as I have tried to show, all stories are bound by

[2] Most theologians, unfortunately, are *not* of this sort.
[3] *A Separate Reality*, New York, 1971. This idea also bears some resemblance to the Mahayana Buddhist ideal of the Bodhisattva.

these limits. A new story would produce a new meaning—a new sense and reference. A new story would imply a new world and a new self—perhaps a new metaphysics, a changing of the limits—but not an exceeding of limits altogether.

The attempt to exceed the limits requires instead a new word, a resurrected word. There is always the possibility, despite human frailty and finitude, that the word will be resurrected. It happens all the time. Yet it is a terrible emergence, a difficult struggle, and one which the theologian-critic cannot afford to ignore. How is it that the creature can also create? How is it that the word, which derives its power and importance from story, can destroy story? How is it that the word can be resurrected?

The myth of the Garden ends with our damnation into history. There is, however, in the Judeo-Christian tradition another story or group of stories, parabolic fragments scattered here and there, which stand as a sort of mirror-image to the story of the Garden. These stories are sometimes associated with the phrase "the kingdom of God" or "of Heaven." Like the Eden myth, they are also spatial stories; in them the man-made garden to which Adam and Eve were condemned by God paradoxically turns out to be the Garden of Eden, or perhaps something even better than the original Garden, a new garden—or city, as it is sometimes envisioned—in which crime is surpassed by justice and justice is exceeded by mercy, in which dreams come true and truth becomes a dream, in which the paradoxes and (spatial) divisions of the Garden unfold themselves fully and make nonsense out of sense, parable out of myth. In the resurrection of the word, the tragic Garden becomes the comic Kingdom.[4]

The new word may not be an original word, but it is always a resurrected word. It is both non-identical and non-different. I am not here denying that languages have histories, but rather asserting the old paradox of the hermeneutical circle: how can the unfamiliar be expressed in terms of the familiar? The circle resolves itself through a violent sacrifice, in which meaning is established. The "newness" of the word is its ability to resist meaning, to reject our attempts to grasp and possess it—its resurrection. In this resurrection and rejection of meaning, we see the fundamental negativity of creativity, to which Sartre, Ingarden,

---

[4] Cf. Crossan, 1976, 1980. In *Theology as Comedy*, I explore the notion that theology might be fundamentally comic.

Jakobson, Crossan, and many others have pointed. Through the resurrection of the word, the limits of story can be exceeded.

2. Theology and Dada

> Dada is a state of mind. That is why it transforms itself according to races and events. Dada applies itself to everything and yet it is nothing, it is the point where the yes and the no and all the opposites meet, not solemnly in the castles of human philosophies, but very simply at street corners, like dogs and grasshoppers.
> Like everything in life, Dada is useless.
> Dada is without pretension, as life should be.
> Perhaps you will understand me better when I tell you that Dada is a virgin microbe that penetrates with the insistence of air into all the space that reason has not been able to fill with words or conventions.[5]
>
> The transparent skin of man allows one to gaze closely upon his soul. There within him it twitches, jerks and beats, as he contentedly lolls around with his clock-work, framework and canals. The red, yellow and blue cords which perform the twitching, jerking and beating, intensify the horror that grips the observer at the sight of any living body. Therefore let us rather depict from now on the anatomy of complexity and unreality that is our flaky being primitively like the folds on the robes of saints of old. . . .
> Eternity smokes joy and suffering out of us as from pipes. We are compensated by the dream, by a good drink. In big draughts we swill down the dream, until the day shrilly awakes us and tears us from the other world. Helpless and terrified we must rise up again in this world. In a few eyes hangs the darkness of the theatre-boxes with their little erotic expedients. But behind nature's flowers rings on the song of the women in labour. (Arp in Last: 72–73)

In Chapter One, I spoke of self-referential* art and literature as a sort of Dada. Sixty to seventy years ago, Tristan Tzara, Hans Arp, and other Dadaists were calling for a "concrete art," characterized by anonymous, "direct" creation, as opposed to an imitation of or abstraction from nature. "These [concrete] works . . . seek to attain the transcendent, the eternal which lies

---

[5] Tristan Tzara, "Lecture on Dada," trans. by Robert Motherwell.

above and beyond the human" (75). They reject convention and
have no descriptive content.

> 'Concretion' describes the natural processes of concen-
> tration, solidification, coagulation, thickening, growing
> together. 'Concretion' describes the process of the
> hardening of a mass. . . . Everything that exists is 'con-
> cretion' and therefore art is too, but art tends to distance
> itself from nature, and this rift, this tragic split I call
> 'human.' (77)

The Dadaists have not somehow escaped from the metaphysics of presence. "Only the spirit, the dream, art, lead to true
collaboration. Such playing leads men to the true life" (80). Platonic and neo-Platonic tendencies, as well as overtones of Freud
and Bergson, among others, cannot be ignored. Nonetheless, the
notion of concrete art as the rejection of meaning, the object
which escapes the enclosure, unsettles even the metaphysics of
Dada.[6] Arp quotes Hugo Ball: "Christ is word and image. The
word and the image have been crucified" (79). The resurrected
word is a concrete word, and it requires a concrete theology.

The rejection of logocentrism in Dada reaches its limit in the
phenomena of "sound-poetry" and *lettrisme*. In sound-poetry,
according to Ball:

> You withdraw into the inmost alchemy of the word.
> Then let the word be sacrificed as well, so as to preserve
> for poetry its last and holiest domain. Give up the crea-
> tion of poetry at second-hand: namely the adoption of
> words (to say nothing of sentences) which are not
> immaculately new and invented for your own use.
> (Quoted in Steiner: 194)

This "poetry without words" is "onomatopoeic foolery" (195),
vocal utterance which is without sense, yet it can be identified as
poetry. The *lettrist* poem, similarly, breaks the written word
down into letters, perhaps from a variety of alphabets, and
arranges them in a poetic but actually unspeakable order.
Steiner comments:

6 "[The] ambiguous object confronts aesthetic activity with an incompletable
task because in its contingency it remains aesthetically indifferent, and thus it
holds open the possibility that a new *objet trouvé* will ask in different terms
under what conditions an isolated object can become art and consequently the
aesthetic become an event . . ." (Jauss: 605).

> The result is a disturbing sensation of possible events and
> densities (Heidegger's *Dichtung*) just below the visual
> surface. No signals . . . are allowed to emerge and evoke
> a familiar tonal context. Yet there is no doubt in my
> mind that we are looking at a poem, and that it is, in
> some way, oddly moving. The wall is at the same time
> blank and expressive. (196)

We are at, or perhaps a little beyond, the level of "nonsense"
discussed in Chapter One. The "concrete poets" are creating at
(or at least near) the level of the material, hyletic phase of the
sign. At this level, translation is both entirely impossible and
entirely unnecessary; we appear to be very close to Benjamin's
notion of a "pure language." At the opposite extreme, the ideal
of an objectively referential scientific discourse, a *Begriffsschrift*,
translation is both possible and necessary. It is in between these
extremes—i.e. in actual stories in actual languages—that translation is a problem.

In concrete poetry, the new, resurrected word is caught in the
act of coming into being; it is on the metaphysical border, between
chaos and sense. It is not the Heideggerian "primordial word." The
concrete word is rather the "primordial non-presence" of the word
(Derrida, 1973:82), the material incarnation which is sacrificed to
(forgotten in) meaning. It is completely "literal" and senseless. It is
the disseminated word, the differance of sense disrupted by the
sign, in contrast to the polysemic word, the differance of reference
disrupted by sense.

Whether the poet truly creates the new word or simply assists
at its "birth" cannot be considered here. The theologian, however,
is not as such a poet or an artist, but a critic. His or her job, then, is
not to create (to resurrect) the new word, but to recognize it, insofar as the non-identical can be recognized—to seek its traces in the
weave of language, and to refuse the decisive and violent sacrifice
which meaning demands. The theologian is a human being and
therefore cannot exist without making decisions. "Concrete theology" would appear then to be amoral and even anti-human, not
unlike the Dadaists and modern deconstructionists. Should we not
expect such an appearance from anyone seeking to exceed the
limits, for whatever reason? One might be tempted to say that
such theology would bring belief to an end, for have we not seen
that belief is the sacrificial decision itself? However, so long as
theology—or any criticism—must continue to operate in and with

words (such as these) and so long as theological language remains meaningful criticism and not concrete poetry, some vestige of belief must remain. We approach the end without end. Self-referential literature is an atheism of the word, but critical disciplines can never become entirely self-referential. (As he readily admits, even Derrida remains bound to logocentrism.)

We use words in two different ways. We use words to fill in the silences or the blank spaces in reality with meaning; we lie, telling stories belonging to the first two genres described in Chapter Four. We eliminate the holes in reality, the discontinuities and incompletenesses, the unenclosed spaces. Or we may use words to structure the emptinesses and refer to the holes, to make the silence audible and the blankness visible—not directly, of course, for that would be self-contradictory, but paradoxically, with the circumlocutions of the mystic. We say it without saying it; this is the third story genre noted in Chapter Four. The first two genres reflect in their violence our fear and pride, and therefore they are tragic and moral genres; the third one reflects our doubt[7] and humility, and therefore it is comic and amoral. The first two are mythic, and the third one is parabolic. "Concrete theology" discovers the parabolic within the mythic: the doubt within fear, and the humility within pride. It finds meaningless meaning: meaning that has been emptied of its meaning.

Concrete theology is therefore mystical, in its way. It is also materialistic. It hungers and thirsts for "the things themselves": the senseless, hyletic phase of the sign, the "that" of the word itself. It seeks oblivion: the nullification of self and world and the discovery of an undecidable oscillation of within and without, content and context. It knows no other world, no Absolute Signified; only "this" and nothing else.

However, concrete theology is not a return to the Dada movement of sixty years ago. It finds in that movement, with its fearless approach to the chaos that surrounds us and the sacrifices that we make in order to give sense to our existence, an analogy to a similar fearlessness in theology, while it seeks to

---

[7] The belief required by this third genre is self-referential and non-identical, and therefore it is impossible without doubt. This may remind us of Paul Tillich's "Protestant Principle," and of existentialism in general. On "two types of writing," see Derrida, 1978:265ff.

comprehend its own chaos—perhaps the "same" chaos? It is not
the way out of the chaos; no theology is capable of that. It is
rather a way of surviving, of "going on" and "keeping one's
head" while passing through this time of the end of metaphysics.

The mythic structures of our day have come apart. They
still are coming apart, crumbling and splintering and crashing
down upon the ground of our despair. It is a surprisingly silent
fall, which though itself unheard yet echoes through the ages—
the slow-motion disintegration of the gods. All that we have left
are the fragments of yesterday's firm conviction—here an arm,
there a head, somewhere else a torso. What we mistook for a
shaking of the foundations was an earthquake tearing apart the
very substance of our logocentric, onto-theological world. Not
only has God died, but as Foucault has noted, even "man"
remains only as a vestige of an age long surpassed, increasingly
incomprehensible and unacceptable (1970:386–87). In such a
world, hermeneutics is de-constructed, and the fragments of
reality, the work of art, the word, can only stand and be experienced "by themselves," in their material senselessness. And yet,
as we have seen, the hyletic can only be "experienced" as chaos.
Questions of reality and meaning can no longer be asked; the
mythic framework is shattered. At the end of metaphysics lie
aphorisms and parables.

Concrete theology cannot be systematic theology. Dada pro-
claims the futility of systems; it exists only in the bits and pieces,
broken fragments, jagged edges. It seeks out the holes and
emptinesses, the silences and blank spaces that appear when the
world becomes too large to fill and too chaotic to organize.
Therefore, deconstruction cannot be yet another philosophical
vehicle in the long series of metaphysical structures upon which
theology has been carried; indeed, it is deconstruction which
uncovers the dissystematicity of those systematic vehicles, and
therefore also the incoherence hidden within the theologies
which depended upon them. Concrete theology as a deconstructive theology must reveal its proper non-presence in the dispersed materiality and violence of inscription, in a dissemination
beyond the metaphysics of historical univocity or structural
polysemy, in a fundamental (but never original) undecidability.
Could theology ever exceed the metaphysics of a canon?
". . . there will never be . . . any theology of the Text" (Derrida,
1981:258). In order to exceed the limits, theology must uncover

the not-itself which lies unnamed at its center, its hidden eccentricity and non-identity: it must become concrete.

3. An Invitation

Like all books, this one must end; it must come to a final word. I would hope, however, for an "end without end," which would be, among other things, an indication of limits. At the end of Chapter One, I spoke of the essential incompleteness of this work, its self-limitation, and I invited the reader to explore further the questions and answers offered here. I do so again. I spoke of this book as a series of approximations of an ultimately indefinable object; approximations call for continuing refinement.

I conceive of three forms that such refinement might take. First, a number of more or less unsupported assertions have been made, which call for evidence. Because this work is primarily theoretical in focus, very few specific stories have been considered, and then only as illustrations, not as evidence. Second, numerous aspects of these theories—and other closely related theories—have been given very slight treatment. There are no doubt other equally important theoretical questions which have been entirely and perhaps unwisely ignored. Perhaps there are important questions which the theories advocated here do not even permit us to ask, or to conceptualize? Third, the interplay between these theories and some other theories of story has not been considered. However, nothing said in this book should be taken as implying that these theories should replace other approaches to the study of story, although they must of course raise questions about the metaphysics hidden within those approaches. The study of story lies at the intersection of a number of diverse academic disciplines. The theories presented here must therefore interact not only with other theories of story, but with any other relevant theories which are reflective of those disciplines.

The ineffables of story are two: the material sign and the beholder. Yet although we cannot speak or read the sign in its materiality, the text is impossible without it. This is also true, but in a different way, of the beholder. Out of the encounter and conflict—subjection and resistance—of these ineffables comes all that is speakable and readable. It is my hope that this book will be understandable and thought-provoking. Yet the very comprehensibility of this book must be, paradoxically, its most serious limitation.

GLOSSARY

Insofar as it attempts a univocal translation of the following terms and phrases, this Glossary exemplifies the sort of metaphysical inevitability described in this book.

Actant: structural role or function made possible by the construction of narrative; a logical operation to be filled by a specific character or characters (Güttgemanns).

Asemy, asemic: meaningless (neither sense nor reference); nonsignifying. At the limit of the hyletic.

Concretization: the supplementation, in reading, of the incompleteness/indeterminacy of fictional language, so that the illusion of spatio-temporal reality is created. The story as a meaningful object, "incarnate" (Ingarden).

Deconstruct, deconstruction: to uncover and explore the metaphor or non-identity within an ostensibly self-identical (metaphysical) system.

Defamiliarize, defamiliarization: the (thematic or structural) tendency of narrative to move counter to the (implied or actual) reader's expectations; a disruption of the frame.

Differance: "a *sameness* which is not *identical*"; "the *play* of differences" (Derrida, 1973:129, 130; Derrida's emphases). The non-presence of the written word; the metaphoricity which is fundamental to (and which disrupts fundamentally) the metaphysics of presence. The continual need for a supplement, which is interpretation.

Discursive formation: a field of linguistic options; a system of rules which permits or forces statements of a given type or types to appear during a given period (Foucault).

Dissemination: the hyletic limit of writing, without the intention of an author to "rescue" it; thus the necessity of an endless series of repetitions or re-readings, in lieu of an authoritative interpretation. The inevitability of misinterpretation (Derrida).

Divergent infinite series: a formula or system which is in principle incompleteable because always dependent upon some prerequisite, and itself potentially incompleteable, formula (Frege).

Doxic: referring to an existential assertion, an act of belief (Husserl, Derrida).

Episteme: ". . . the totality of relations that can be discovered, for a given period, between the sciences when one analyzes them at the level of discursive regularities" (Foucault, 1972:191).

Epochē: the phenomenological reduction; the suspension of affirmation/belief or denial. To refuse to assign a truth-value (Husserl).

Equivalence: "similarity and dissimilarity, synonymity and antonymity" (Jakobson: 358). Belonging to the "axis of selection" (the paradigm); essential to the metaphoricity of the poetic function.

Excess: the non-metaphysical, as that residue which cannot be contained in any possible presence, in the "closure" of metaphysics—as in a divergent infinite series. The superfluity of writing within the metaphysics of presence (Derrida).

Fable (*fabula*): the order of events (in reality or fantasy) to which the story refers; what "actually" happens, as a determinant of the sense of a story.

Horizon: a "background" of potential meaning (Ingarden: 219). The limits of the world, as established by a particular consciousness or story; the margin of that which is "co-present" (Husserl, Gadamer).

Hylē, hyletic: the material stuff of the sign, as (logically) distinct from any interpretation of it. The material phase of any phenomenon, essential to any consciousness, but never experienced as such, or apart from its intentional form (noesis) (Husserl).

Implied author: narrative structure determining referentiality; illusion (or "second self") of an author; "the norm of the work" (Chatman: 149; Booth).

Implied dialog: story as communication between an implied author and implied reader, as well as the "narrator" (if any) and characters of the story. Determinant of "aesthetic distance" (Booth).

Implied reader: narrative structure determining referentiality; illusion (or "second self") of a reader; counterpart of the implied author. The "postulated reader" (Booth: 157; Chatman).

Jewel-case: one of many Derridean metaphors for writing, in this case a "volume" which opens and shuts (and therefore enfolds and encloses metaphysically), and therefore a womb (the Platonic Cave of illusion/representation) protected by a membrane (hymen/texture/weaving = page) and penetrated violently by the spur (phallus/point = pen) of writing.

Logocentrism: the (Western) metaphysics of presence, of which the originality of the spoken word is the central metaphor; ". . . the privilege of the logos" (Derrida, 1976: 285). See "onto-theology."

Mega-metaphor: the metaphor of metaphor; a metaphor explaining or interpreting other metaphors. The infinite regression of linguistic incompleteness. A metaparable; analogous to "meta-story" (Crossan).

Mergence: the artificial uniting or reconciling of spatial difference through juxtaposition within a map; the integration of logical oppositions (Vernon).

Metaphor: in a broad sense, any figure (or trope) of language, in which language resists our desire to possess it through a single, identical framing of sense and reference; the fundamental incompleteness of language.

Meta-story: a story about stories, or a story in terms of which other stories are judged, interpreted, etc. Also: meta-belief, meta-ethics, meta-genre, meta-language.

Motif: the concrete realization in a narrative of the opposition of motifemes, through characters in action (Güttgemanns, Crossan).

Motifeme: ". . . a proposition in which an actant is predicatively associated with an act" (Güttgemanns: 52). A function within a structure determined by binary logic (Crossan).

Noema, noematic: the meaning or object intended by consciousness. The referent signified by the sign (Husserl).

Noesis, noetic: the formal dimension of the intending consciousness. The sign as a signifier (Husserl).

Non-present: neither present nor absent (or alternatively, both present and absent). Non-metaphysical; non-identical.

Opalescent multiplicity: the ambiguity of terms or phrases which is essential to fictional language; also, the "loose connection" between such ambiguous language and unequivocal statements (Ingarden).

Onto-theology: the metaphysics of the Western tradition, for which presence (= self-identity, = being) is primary. The forgetting of differance, which is surpassed by differance (Heidegger, Derrida).

Plot (sjužet): the (written or spoken) order of events in a narrative; sequence of words, or syntagm. How the story is told, as a determinant of its sense.

Reconstruction: that which replaces (and displaces) metaphysics, for which deconstruction is to prepare the way. The surpassing of the fundamental undecidability of differance (Raschke).

Self-referentiality: the disruption of the metaphysical referentiality of narrative as a result of the infinite regression of (and reversal within) content and context; the non-identity of sense.

Spots of indeterminancy: the lack of unequivocal determinability of an infinite manifold of properties, aspects, etc. which characterizes any fictional object, "overlooked" in the act of reading (Ingarden).

Surplus: the overflowing of meaning in discourse; metaphor conceived as presence which surpasses all metaphysical limits (Ricoeur).

Unsaturated function: an incomplete thought or statement, containing "empty places," which must be filled (supplemented) by properly-referential terms in order that it may have a sense; a non-referring predicate (Frege).

BIBLIOGRAPHY

Alexander, Ronald G.
1978   *Ricoeur's View of the Meaning of a
                        Text*. Paper presented to Upper
                        Midwest regional meeting, American
                        Academy of Religion, April, 1978.
Altizer, Thomas J. J., Max A. Myers, Carl A. Raschke, Robert P.
Scharlemann, Mark C. Taylor, and Charles E. Winquist
1982   *Deconstruction and Theology*. New
                        York: The Crossroad Publishing Co.
Aristotle
1926   *The Art of Rhetoric*. John Henry
                        Freese, trans. Cambridge, Mass.:
                        Harvard Univ. Press.
1941   *On Interpretation*. E. M. Edghill,
                        trans., in *The Basic Works of Aristotle*.
                        Richard McKeon, ed. New York:
                        Random House.
1947   *Poetics*. Ingram Bywater, trans., in
                        Introduction to Aristotle. Richard
                        McKeon, ed. New York: The Modern
                        Library.
Arnheim, Rudolf
1978   "A Stricture on Space and Time."
                        Critical Inquiry 4: 645–55.
Bachelard, Gaston
1964   *The Poetics of Space*. Maria Jolas, trans.
                        Boston: The Beacon Press.
1969   *The Poetics of Reverie*. Daniel Russell,
                        trans. Boston: The Beacon Press.

Barfield, Owen
1964   *Poetic Diction: A Study in Meaning.*
                            New York: McGraw-Hill Book Co.
1977   *The Rediscovery of Meaning, and
                            Other Essays.* Middletown, Conn.:
                            Wesleyan Univ. Press.
Barthes, Roland
1979   "From Work to Text." In *Textual
                            Strategies.* Josué V. Harari, trans. and
                            ed. Ithaca, NY: Cornell Univ. Press.
Benjamin, Walter
1968   *Illuminations.* Harry Zohn, trans. New
                            York: Schocken Books.
Bentham, Jeremy
1959   *The Theory of Fictions.* C. K. Ogden,
                            ed. Paterson, NJ: Littlefield, Adams, and
                            Co.
Bergson, Henri
1900   "Laughter." In *Comedy.* Wylie Sypher,
                            ed. Garden City, NY: Doubleday and
                            Co., Inc.
1949   *Selections from Bergson.* Harold A.
                            Larrabee, ed. New York: Appleton-
                            Century-Crofts, Inc.
1955   *An Introduction to Metaphysics.* T. E.
                            Hulme, trans. Indianapolis, Ind.: The
                            Bobbs-Merrill Co., Inc.
Boomershine, Thomas E.
1980   "The Structure of Narrative Rhetoric in
                            Genesis 2–3." *Semeia* 18: 113–29.
Booth, Wayne C.
1961   *The Rhetoric of Fiction.* Chicago: Univ.
                            of Chicago Press.
Borges, Jorge Luis
1962   *Ficciones.* Anthony Kerrigan, trans.
                            New York: The Grove Press, Inc.

Buckman, Thomas R.
1966   "Introduction." In *Modern Theatre.*
                       Thomas R. Buckman, ed. Lincoln, Neb.:
                       Univ. of Nebraska Press.

Bultmann, Rudolf
1963   *History of the Synoptic Tradition.* John
                       Marsh, trans. New York: Harper & Row.

Calloud, Jean
1976   *Structural Analysis of Narrative.* Daniel
                       Patte, trans. Philadelphia/Missoula,
                       Mont.: Fortress Press/Scholars Press.

Camus, Albert
1956   *The Fall.* Justin O'Brien, trans. New
                       York: Random House.

Cannon, Dale W.
1975   "Ruminations on the Claim of
                       Inenarrability." *Journal of the
                       American Academy of Religion* 43:
                       560–85.

Castaneda, Hector-Neri
1978   "Fiction and Reality: Their
                       Fundamental Connections." Paper read
                       at lecture presented by the Univ. of
                       Michigan Philosophy Dept., October,
                       1978.

Chatman, Seymour
1978   *Story and Discourse.* Ithaca, NY:
                       Cornell Univ. Press.

Crossan, John Dominic
1973   *In Parables.* New York: Harper & Row.
1974   "Parable and Example in the Teaching
                       of Jesus," and "Structuralist Analysis and
                       the Parables of Jesus." *Semeia* 1: 63–104
                       and 192–221.
1975   *The Dark Interval: Towards a Theology
                       of Story.* Niles, Ill.: Argus
                       Communications.
1976   *Raid on the Articulate.* New York:
                       Harper & Row.

1979   *Finding Is the First Act.* Philadelphia/
                Missoula, Mont.: Fortress Press/Scholars
                Press.
1980a   *Cliffs of Fall.* New York: Seabury Press.
1980b   "Felix Culpa and Foenix Culprit."
                Semeia 18: 107–11.
1982   "Difference and Divinity." *Semeia* 23:
                29–40.

Deleuze, Gilles
1979   "The Schizophrenic and Language:
                Surface and Depth in Lewis Carroll and
                Antonin Artaud." In *Textual Strategies.*
                Josué V. Harari, trans. and ed. Ithaca,
                NY: Cornell Univ. Press.

de Man, Paul
1978   "The Epistemology of Metaphor." In *On
                Metaphor.* Sheldon Sacks, ed. Chicago:
                Univ. of Chicago Press.
1979   "Shelley Disfigured." In *Deconstruction
                and Criticism.* New York: The Seabury
                Press.

Derrida, Jacques
1973   *Speech and Phenomena.* David B.
                Allison, trans. Evanston, Ill.:
                Northwestern Univ. Press.
1976   *Of Grammatology.* Gayatri
                Chakravorty Spivak, trans. Baltimore:
                The Johns Hopkins Univ. Press.
1978   *Writing and Difference.* Alan Bass,
                trans. Chicago: Univ of Chicago Press.
1979   *Spurs: Nietzsche's Styles.* Barbara
                Harlow, trans. Chicago: Univ. of
                Chicago Press.
1980   "The Law of Genre." Avital Ronell,
                trans. *Glyph* 7: 176–229.
1981   *Dissemination.* Barbara Johnson, trans.
                Chicago: Univ. of Chicago Press.

1982
"Letter to John P. Leavey, Jr." and "Of an Apocalyptic Tone Recently Adopted in Philosophy." John P. Leavey, Jr., trans. *Semeia* 23: 61–97.

Detweiler, Robert
1978
Story, Sign, and Self. Philadelphia/Missoula, Mont.: Fortress Press/Scholars Press.

Dibelius, Martin
n.d.
From Tradition to Gospel. Bertram Lee Woolf, trans. New York: Charles Scribner's Sons.

Dunne, John S.
1977
A Search for God in Time and Memory. Notre Dame, Ind.: Univ. of Notre Dame Press.

Eliot, T. S.
1964
"Tradition and the Individual Talent." In *Selected Essays.* New York: Harcourt, Brace, and World, Inc.

Emrich, Wilhelm
1968
Franz Kafka. Sheema Zeben Buehne, trans. New York: Ungar Publishing Co.

Estess, Ted L.
1974
"The Inenarrable Contraption: Reflections on the Metaphor of Story." *Journal of the American Academy of Religion* 42: 415–34.

Fackenheim, Emil L.
1970
God's Presence in History. New York: Harper & Row.

Flew, Antony, and Alasdair MacIntyre
1955
New Essays in Philosophical Theology. London: SCM Press Ltd.

Foucault, Michel
1970
The Order of Things. A. Sheridan Smith, trans. New York: Random House.

1972   *The Archaeology of Knowledge* and *The Discourse on Language*. A. M. Sheridan Smith and Rupert Sawyer, trans. New York: Harper & Row.

1979   "What Is an Author?" In *Textual Strategies*. Josué V. Harari, trans. and ed. Ithaca, NY: Cornell Univ. Press.

Frank, Joseph

1963   *The Widening Gyre*. New Brunswick, NJ: Rutgers Univ. Press.

1977   "Spatial Form: An Answer to Critics." *Critical Inquiry* 4: 231–52.

1978   "Spatial Form: Some Further Reflections." *Critical Inquiry* 5: 276–90.

Frege, Gottlob

1952   *Translations From the Writings of Gottlob Frege*. P. T. Geach and M. Black, trans. and ed. Totowa, NJ: Rowman and Littlefield.

Frye, Northrop

1957   *Anatomy of Criticism*. Princeton, NJ: Princeton Univ. Press.

1963a   *Fables of Identity*. New York: Harcourt, Brace, and World, Inc.

1963b   *The Well-Tempered Critic*. Bloomington, Ind.: Indiana Univ. Press.

1976   "History and Myth in the Bible." In *The Literature of Fact*. Angus Fletcher, ed. New York: Columbia Univ. Press.

Gadamer, Hans-Georg

1975   *Truth and Method*. Garrett Barden and John Cumming, trans. New York: The Seabury Press.

1976   *Philosophical Hermeneutics*. David Linge, trans. and ed. Berkeley and Los Angeles: Univ. of California Press.

Gerhart, Mary
1977   "Generic Studies: Their Renewed
                       Importance in Religious and Literary
                       Interpretation." *Journal of the
                       American Academy of Religion* 45:
                       309–25.

Girard, René
1977   *Violence and the Sacred.* Patrick
                       Gregory, trans. Baltimore: The Johns
                       Hopkins Univ. Press.

Glatzer, Nahum N.
1958   "Franz Kafka and the Tree of
                       Knowledge." *Between East and West*:
                       48–58.

Gödel, Kurt
1930   "Some Metamathematical Results on
                       Completeness and Consistency." In
                       *From Frege to Gödel: A Source Book of
                       Mathematical Logic, 1897–1931.* Jan
                       van Heijenoort, ed. Cambridge, Mass.:
                       Harvard Univ. Press.

Graff, Gerald
1979   *Literature Against Itself.* Chicago:
                       Univ. of Chicago Press.
1980   *Poetic Statement and Critical Dogma.*
                       Chicago: Univ. of Chicago Press.

Greenberg, Martin
1965   *The Terror of Art.* New York: Basic
                       Books.

Güttgemanns, Erhardt
1976   *Generative Poetics.* William G. Doty,
                       trans. The entire issue of *Semeia* 6.

Hauerwas, Stanley
1977   *Truthfulness and Tragedy.* Some
                       chapters co-authored by Richard Bondi
                       or David B. Burrell. Notre Dame, Ind.:
                       Univ. of Notre Dame Press.

Heidegger, Martin
1971a   *On the Way to Language.* Peter D.
                         Hertz, trans. New York: Harper & Row.
1971b   *Poetry, Language, Thought.* Albert
                         Hofstadter, trans. New York: Harper &
                         Row.
1972   *On Time and Being.* Joan Stambaugh,
                         trans. New York: Harper & Row.

Hernadi, Paul
1972   *Beyond Genre, New Directions In
                         Literary Classification*, Ithaca, NY:
                         Cornell Univ. Press.

Hirsch, E. D., Jr.
1967   *Validity in Interpretation.* New Haven,
                         Conn.: Yale Univ. Press.

Holtz, William
1977   "Spatial Form in Modern Literature: A
                         Reconsideration." *Critical Inquiry* 4:
                         271–83.

Hulme, T. E.
1954   *Speculations.* London: Routledge and
                         Kegan Paul Ltd.

Hume, David
1977   *An Enquiry Concerning Human
                         Understanding.* Indianapolis: Hackett
                         Publishing Co.

Husserl, Edmund
1962   *Ideas.* W. R. Boyce Gibson, trans. New
                         York: Macmillan Publishing Co.

Ingarden, Roman
1973   *The Literary Work of Art.* George G.
                         Grabowicz, trans. Evanston, Ill.:
                         Northwestern Univ. Press.

The Interpreter's Bible
1952   *Genesis.* New York and Nashville,
                         Tenn.: Abingdon-Cokesbury Press.

Jakobson, Roman
1960 "Linguistics and Poetics." In *Style in Language*. Thomas A. Sebeok, ed. Cambridge, Mass.: M.I.T. Press.

James, William
1909 "The Function of Cognition." In *Pragmatism and Four Essays from the Meaning of Truth*. New York: The New American Library, Inc.

Jauss, Hans Robert
1982 "Poiesis." Michael Shaw, trans. *Critical Inquiry* 8: 591–608.

Jeremias, Joachim
1963 *The Parables of Jesus*. S. H. Hooke, trans. London: SCM Press Ltd.

Jobling, David
1980 "The Myth Semantics of Genesis 2:4b-3:24." *Semeia* 18: 41–49.

Jung, L. Shannon
1982 "Spatiality, Relativism, and Authority." *Journal of the American Academy of Religion* 50: 215–35.

Kafka, Franz
1946 *Parables and Paradoxes*. New York: Schocken Books.

Kant, Immanuel
1951 *Critique of Judgment*. J. H. Bernard, trans. New York: Hafner Press.

Kliever, Lonnie D.
1977 "Story and Space: the Forgotten Dimension." *Journal of the American Academy of Religion* 45: 529–63.

Köhler, Ludwig
1957 *Old Testament Theology*. A. S. Todd, trans. Philadelphia: The Westminster Press.

Kort, Wesley A.
1975 *Narrative Elements and Religious Meaning*. Philadelphia: Fortress Press.

Lagerkvist, Pär
1951   *Barabbas.* Alan Blair, trans. New York:
                             Random House.
1958   *The Sibyl.* Naomi Walford, trans. New
                             York: Random House.
1966   "Modern Theatre: Points of View and
                             Attack." In *Modern Theatre.* Thomas R.
                             Buckman, trans. and ed. Lincoln, Neb.:
                             Univ. of Nebraska Press.
Lakoff, George, and Mark Johnson
1980   *Metaphors We Live By.* Chicago: Univ.
                             of Chicago Press.
Last, R. W., trans. and ed.
1969   *Hans Arp, The Poet of Dadaism.*
                             London: Oswald Wolff.
Leavey, John P., Jr.
1982   "Four Protocols: Derrida, His
                             Deconstruction." *Semeia* 23: 42–57.
Lévi-Strauss, Claude
1958   "The Structural Study of Myth." In
                             Myth: A Symposium. Thomas A.
                             Sebeok, ed. Bloomington, Ind.: Indiana
                             Univ. Press.
Malraux, André
1978   *The Voices of Silence.* Stuart Gilbert,
                             trans. Princeton, NJ: Princeton Univ.
                             Press.
Maritain, Jacques
1962   *A Preface to Metaphysics.* New York:
                             New American Library.
Mitchell, W. J. T.
1980   "Spatial Form in Literature: Toward a
                             General Theory." *Critical Inquiry* 6:
                             539–67.
1981   "Diagrammatology." *Critical Inquiry* 7:
                             622–33.

Nietzsche, Friedrich
1955   *Beyond Good and Evil.* Marianne
                       Cowan, trans. Chicago: Henry Regnery
                       Co.
Patte, Daniel, and Judson F. Parker
1980   "A Structural Exegesis of Genesis 2–3."
                       Semeia 18: 55–75.
Phillips, Gary
1980   "Structure and Narration, An
                       Enunciative View." *Semeia* 18: 131–35.
Plato
1956   *Symposium.* Benjamin Jowett, trans.
                       Indianapolis, Ind.: The Bobbs-Merrill
                       Co., Inc.
1959   *Timaeus.* Francis M. Cornford, trans.
                       Indianapolis, Ind.: The Bobbs-Merrill
                       Co., Inc.
1973   *Phaedrus, and Letters VII and VIII.*
                       Walter Hamilton, trans. Middlesex,
                       Eng.: Penguin Books.
1973   *The Republic and Other Works.* B.
                       Jowett, trans. Garden City, NY:
                       Doubleday.
Rabkin, Eric S.
1977   "Spatial Form and Plot." *Critical
                       Inquiry* 4: 253–70.
Raschke, Carl A.
1979   *The Alchemy of the Word: Language
                       and the End of Theology.* Missoula,
                       Mont.: Scholars Press.
Richards, I. A.
1929   *Practical Criticism.* New York:
                       Harcourt, Brace, and Co.
1964   *The Philosophy of Rhetoric.* Oxford:
                       Oxford Univ. Press.
Ricoeur, Paul
1976   *Interpretation Theory.* Fort Worth,
                       Texas: The T.C.U. Press.

1977   *The Rule of Metaphor.* R. Czerny, K.
                McLaughlin, and J. Costello, trans.
                Toronto: Univ. of Toronto Press.
1978a   "The Metaphorical Process as Cognition,
                Imagination, and Feeling." In *On
                Metaphor.* Sheldon Sacks, ed. Chicago:
                Univ. of Chicago Press.
1978b   "The Narrative Function." *Semeia* 13:
                177–202.
1980   "Narrative Time." *Critical Inquiry* 7:
                169–90.
Rorty, Richard
1979   *Philosophy and the Mirror of Nature.*
                Princeton, NJ: Princeton Univ. Press.
Said, Edward W.
1978   "The Problem of Textuality: Two
                Exemplary Positions." *Critical Inquiry*
                4: 673–714.
Sartre, Jean-Paul
n.d.   *The Psychology of Imagination.*
                Secaucus, NJ: Citadel Press.
1956   *Being and Nothingness.* Hazel Barnes,
                trans. New York: Philosophical Library,
                Inc.
1963   *Search for a Method.* Hazel E. Barnes,
                trans. New York: Random House.
Scholes, Robert
1974   *Structuralism in Literature.* New
                Haven, Conn.: Yale Univ. Press.
1980   "Language, Narrative, and Anti-
                Narrative." *Critical Inquiry* 7: 204–12.
Scholes, Robert and Robert Kellogg
1966   *The Nature of Narrative.* New York:
                Oxford Univ. Press.
Scruton, Roger
1981   *From Descartes to Wittgenstein.* New
                York: Harper & Row.

Spector, Robert Donald
1973   *Pär Lagerkvist.* New York: Twayne
                    Publishers, Inc.
Steiner, George
1975   *After Babel.* Oxford: Oxford Univ.
                    Press.
Strauss, Walter A.
1961   "Franz Kafka: Between the Paradise
                    and the Labyrinth." In *Centennial
                    Review of Arts and Sciences,* Vol. 5.
                    East Lansing, Mich.: Michigan State
                    Univ.
Surette, Leon
1981   "Rational Form in Literature." *Critical
                    Inquiry* 7: 612–21.
Swanson, Roy Authur
1966   "Evil and Love in Lagerkvist's
                    Crucifixion Cycle." *Scandinavian
                    Studies* 38: 302–17.
Tillich, Paul
1959   *Theology of Culture.* New York: Oxford
                    Univ. Press.
Todorov, Tzvetan
1973   *The Fantastic.* Richard Howard, trans.
                    Cleveland: Case Western Reserve Univ.
                    Press.
1977   *The Poetics of Prose.* Richard Howard,
                    trans. Ithaca, NY: Cornell Univ. Press.
Tolkien, J. R. R.
1966   "On Fairy-Stories." In *Essays Presented
                    to Charles Williams.* C. S. Lewis, ed.
                    Grand Rapids, Mich.: Wm. B. Eerdmans
                    Publishing Co.
Tracy, David
1978   "Metaphor and Religion: the Test Case
                    of Christian Texts." In *On Metaphor.*
                    Sheldon Sacks, ed. Chicago: Univ. of
                    Chicago Press.

158   The Limits of Story

Vernon, John
1973   *The Garden and the Map*. Urbana, Ill.:
                        Univ. of Illinois Press.
Via, Dan Otto, Jr.
1967   *The Parables*. Philadelphia: Fortress
                        Press.
1974   "Parable and Example Story: A
                        Literary-Structuralist Approach" and "A
                        Response to Crossan, Funk, and
                        Petersen." *Semeia* 1: 105–33 and
                        222–35.
1975   *Kerygma and Comedy in the New
                        Testament*. Philadelphia: Fortress Press.
1976   "Religion and Story: Of Time and
                        Reality." *The Journal of Religion* 56:
                        392–99.
von Rad, Gerhard
1961   *Genesis*. John H. Marks, trans.
                        Philadelphia: The Westminster Press.
1962   *Old Testament Theology*. Vol. 1.
                        D. M. G. Stalker, trans. New York:
                        Harper & Row.
Weathers, Winston
1968   *Pär Lagerkvist: A Critical Essay*. Grand
                        Rapids, Mich.: Wm. B. Eerdmans
                        Publishing Co.
Wellek, René and Austin Warren
1949   *Theory of Literature*. New York:
                        Harcourt, Brace, and Co.
Westermann, Claus
1974   *Creation*. John J. Scullion, S.J., trans.
                        Philadelphia: Fortress Press.
White, Hugh C.
1980   "Direct and Third Person Discourse in
                        the Narrative of the 'Fall.'" *Semeia* 18:
                        91–106.
Williams, James G.
1980   "The Necessity of Being 'Outside.'"
                        Semeia 18: 51–53.

Wittgenstein, Ludwig
1953   *Philosophical Investigations.* G. E. M.
                       Anscombe, trans. New York: The
                       Macmillan Co.

Wittig, Susan
1977   "A Theory of Multiple Meanings."
                       Semeia 9: 75–103.

Ziolkowski, Theodore
1972   *Fictional Transfigurations of Jesus.*
                       Princeton, NJ: Princeton Univ. Press.

INDEX